3

88-B

DRAMATIC SIGNIFICANCE OF TRAGIC HERO IN SHAKESPEARE

DRAMATIC SIGNIFICANCE OF TRAGIC HERO IN SHAKESPEARE

By
RAVEENDRA KURUP

ANMOL PUBLICATIONS PVT. LTD.
NEW DELHI - 110 002 (INDIA)

ANMOL PUBLICATIONS PVT. LTD.
4374/4B, Ansari Road, Daryaganj
New Delhi - 110 002
Ph.: 3261597, 3278000
Visit us at: www.anmolbooks.com

Dramatic Significance of Tragic Hero in Shakespeare

First Edition, 2003

ISBN 81-261-1408-8

[The responsibility for the facts stated, conclusions reached and plagiarism, if any, in this book is entirely that of the Author. And the Publisher bears no responsibility for them, whatsoever.]

PRINTED IN INDIA

Published by J.L. Kumar for Anmol Publications Pvt. Ltd., New Delhi - 110 002 and Printed at Tarun Offset Printers,

Contents

Preface

My intention in this work has been to study the Dramatic Significance of Tragic Hero in Shakespeare. I have chosen for a detailed analysis of *Hamlet, Macbeth, King Lear* and *Othello* because the dramatic significance and its implications have deeply rooted and involved. The dramatic significance of hero in *Hamlet, Macbeth, Othello* and *King Lear* is thought provoking and keeps a separate identity in the dramatic world. The more we analyse of the tragedies of Shakespeare the dramatic significance of heroes is of high significance. Each hero of Shakespeare is a symbolic one to society. The dashing endeavour of hero in each tragedy of Shakespeare is a matter of great dramatic significance. The purpose of my work is therefore to evaluate the dramatic significance and importance of major tragedies of Shakespeare which undoubtedly stimulates intellectual and academic debate in English literature.

Dr. Raveendra Kurup
M.A. LL.B., Ph.D.

1

Introduction

Aloofness or loneliness has played a vital role in all tragedies of Shakespeare. The heroes are experiences a sense of seapates from soceity. The heroes are subjected to untold ideological clashes. The continuity of clashes is the part and parcel of life of tragic heroes in Shakespeare. When the crises arose the heroes stick up to the same and face the situation courageously and emerges as victorious.

The hero in Shakespeare's major tragedies suffers isolation; he finds himself out of tune with the world that surrounds him and, more poignantly, in opposition to those with whom he had shared love and trust. This seems to us a significant aspect of the tragic situation as presented by Shakespeare, and we propose to study in the following chapters how such a conflict originates and what light it throws on the character of tragic hero.

Isolation as an aspect of the tragic situation is clearly emphasized in *Hamlet, Macbeth, King Lear, Antony and Cleopatra,* and *Coriolaunts.* The hero in each of these tragedies is not only one who is "highly renowned and prosperous," a person of "high degree," but also one who is aware of, an involved in, social and personal relationships. Though the degree of awareness and involvement varies in each case, it may be said with confidence that all these heroes find their identity in the human world, which is the world of all of us, or not at all. What isolates them is their pursuit of identity beyond the socially approved and recognized limits. What matters to the community is obviously social adjustment whereas, as Maynard Mack has pointed out, "what matters to the individual, at least in his heroic mood, is just as obviously integrity--all that enables him to remain an *individual,* one thing not many."[1]

The characters of these heroes vary considerably in their nobility; what they have in common is that they are "exceptional beings." Bradley, while recognizing this, opines that the hero "errs" because of "a fatal tendency to identify the whole being with one interest, object, passion, or habit of mind."[2] There is implicit here a condemnation of the singlemindedness of the hero, though Bradley does seem in his whole argument to be tending toward the assertion Peter Alexander makes--that the tragic *hamartia* takes its character and significance "not from faults but from virtues."[3] The tragic hero possesses virtue, not in the conventional Christian sense, but in the pagan sense--his heroism exhibits itself in strength and intensity of character. His courage in pursuing his search for identity even at the cost of social ostracism is an essentially heroic quality and not a "tragic flaw." The fact that the hero is isolated should not mislead us into thinking that he errs and that the social judgement upon him is right.

Shakespeare's major tragedies present a recurrent pattern of human sacrifice. I agree with his premise that the protagonist in these tragedies pursues a role "which takes him from being the cynosure of his society to being estranged from it," but his conclusion from this, that "what happens to him suggests the expulsion of a scapegoat, or the sacrifice of a victim, or something of both,"[4] seems to me completely unacceptable except in respect of Macbeth and Othello. While it may be true of these two that "weakness easily means isolation,"[5] it is not true of Hamlet, Lear, Antony and

Coriolanus, as is indicated by the frequent qualifications that Holloway has to make in applying the pattern to them.

The difficulty arises because attention is concentrated on the *fact* of isolation rather than on the *significance* of it: that a character is isolated tells us little unless we closely analyse the causes that lead to his isolation, and the nature of his reaction to it. It might, therefore, be useful at this stage to arrange different dramatic presentations of the isolated hero in Shakespeare's major tragedies according to the tragic effect that is created by them:

(a) the isolation of the hero who is 'good' in the sense that "he is the magnified projection of an ideal generally accepted by society."[6] This kind of isolation, which I regard as the most fully tragic, is the consequence of the idealism--the contempt for success at the cost of compromise--that characterizes the hero. He has been, an important member, often a leader, of his society, but in the tragic situation he can retain his stature as a hero only if he refuses the kind of ignoble adjustment that society demands of him. The classic case is that of Hamlet, but--with some differences--Lear, Antony, and Coriolanus also find themselves in similar situations. Each society offers the hero a bribe to persuade him to merge himself with it: Hamlet is offered the place of "chiefest courtier" at Claudius' court; Lear is offered shelter from the storm if he will accept the terms of Goneril and Regan; Antony is married to Octavia to ensure his political subservience to Caesar; and Coriolanus is guaranteed the consulship if he will but flatter the common people by begging their voices. Each of them spurns the bribe and is compelled to stand outside his world. But he does not glory in his state; on the contrary, he regards it as unnatural, an isolation he would willingly end, but not by accepting the compromise that society offers to him. As a result, each of the heroes is exiled from the society to which he belongs. Hamlet is sent to England, Lear's daughters shut their doors against him, Antony's genius is rebuked in the presence of Caesar so he goes to Egypt, and Coriolanus turns to the Volsces when he is banished from Rome.

(b) the second kind of isolation, less obviously tragic than the first, is exemplified by Macbeth. He fully subscribes to the ideals accepted by his society but, by a tragic twist, he is led to desecrate them. The dramatic presentation is correspondingly complex; we witness the spectacle of a man who commits the acts of a criminal but soliloquises over them with a passionate self-awareness which is fully tragic. This demands a sensitive dual response from us; we must at the same time condemn his actions and sympathize with *his own* horror of them. The *fact* of Macbeth's isolation is the same as that of Richard III; what distinguishes them is the reaction to the careers of crime they embark upon.

(c) yet another kind of isolation, that of the hero turned misanthrope, has the appearance of tragedy without its substance. Timon is isolated, but his isolation is meaningless. From his curse

> Burn house ! Sink Arthens ! Henceforth hated be
> Of Timon man and all humanity !
> (*Timon of Athens*, III. vi. I04)

there is no spiritual development to his self-composed epitaph:

> 'Here lie I, Timon, who alive all living men did hate.
> Pass by, and curse thy fill; but pass, and stay not here
> thy gait.'
> (*Timon of Athens*, V. iv. 72)

His ideal of human relationships is too abstractly conceived for us to warm to it. His expectations are of too naive a nature to provide a dramatic framework for any mature exploration of their personal or social relevance. Though Timon is not "determined to be a villain," he lives inasmuch of an emotional vacuum as Richard III does, and a more just epitaph for him would be:

> There is no creature loves me;
> And if I die no soul will pity me:
> And wherefore should they, since that I myself
> Find in myself no pity to myself?
>
> (*Richard III,* V. iii. 200)

(d) the isolation of a hero like Othello, who is conspicuously an alien: this I regard as having more a sociological than a tragic significance. From the first scene to the last, Shakespeare emphasizes the blackness of "The Motor of Venice," and, in this tragedy, the visual impact of the hero's isolation in a stage performance is much more vivid than in the reading of it. The physical difference between Othello and the Venetians is constantly referred to, most poignantly by Othello himself. The tragic situation, of course, is not his isolation from Venetian society, but his loss of faith in Desdemona. But the two are related to his mind; Iago succeeds in making him doubt the fidelity of his wife because he attacks the most vulnerable aspect of his character: his sense of being a man ignorant of the ways of the civilization to which she belongs. Othello is different from the heroes of the other major tragedies in that his position in society is not based on anything more than a contractual arrangement; his social position is, therefore, an insecure one. He holds his palce in Venice at the pleasure of the state, and in fact his command is "taken off" peremptorily in the last scene.

Othello is fundamentally different from the other heroes in his reaction to this social judgement. He makes no attempt to assert his own values which have gone sadly awry in the unfamiliar world of Venice. Shakespeare gives Othello no relationships which his native world. He fetches his "life and being/From men of royal siege" but his ancestry is never really personalized. He has no other ties to fall back upon once he has murdered Desdemona, and been condemned by the Venetian state; he is a rootless man who, before coming to Venice, had lived in an "unhoused free condition." Othello thus has no identity outside Venice, and within it he has a strictly limited one. In the parable with which he ends his life the sociological bias of his tragedy is clear: one who was a Turk and a pagan is compelled to acknowledge that he has failed to become a Venetian and a Christian.

> And say besides that in Aleppo once,
> Where a malignant and a turban'd Turk
> Beat a Venetian and traduc'd the state,
> I took by th' throat the circumcised dog,
> And smote him--thus.
>
> (*Othello,* V. ii. 355)

He completely negates his own identity; what the Venetians in their complacency say about an alien in *The Merchant of Venice* is said here by the alien himself. His death involves no national destinies; he is a foreigner who is discarded by Venice without any social upheaval.

(e) finally, there is an entirely different kind of isolation--that of villains like Claudius and Edmund, who know no loyalty except to their self-interest. Such characters are distinguished by their emotional rootlessness, their nihilistic attitude to the sanctity of human ties, and the obligations that they entail. Claudius and Edmund are the more spectacular examples; there are also their hirelings like Rosencrantz-Guildenstern and Oswald. The group is not limited to men; there are

> also women like Goneril and Regan. It is such characters who undermine the social fabric; it is their "vile offences" which demand their destruction, for otherwise
>
> Humanity must perforce prey on itself,
> Like monsters of the deep.
>
> (*King Lear*, IV. ii. 49)
>
> It is important to distinguish their isolation from that of the heroes. Such characters have no commitment to social and personal relationships; their only interest in these is to exploit them for their own advancement. When this "policy" fails, and they stand exposed as the enemies of society, they express no longing for the sense of community denied to them. Their isolation is a just retribution for their denial of the bond between man and man.

The use of the actor image in the major tragedies is extremely significant in the context of the theme of isolation. The unscrupulous characters, beginning with Claudius, are extremely good actors who can deceive the unsuspecting hero who knows not "seems." The hero is isolated because he cannot compromise his essential principles and pretend to be other than he is; this gives a temporary advantage to the successful hypocrites. The inability to play a part successfully is what elevates Macbeth and Coriolanus to the level of tragic heroes; Antony rises to this stature when he gives up the politic diplomacy that he practises in the first part of the play. The actor image is used not only in a general way, but is particularlyu connected with the use of costume by a stage player. Hamlet's "inky cloak" is, of course, worn in defiance of the festive mood of Claudius' court but he wants to make it clear that he is not using costume as an actor uses it.

> ... I have that within which passes show--
> These but the trappings and the suits of woe.
>
> (*Hamlet*, I. ii. 85)

Macbeth, on the other hand, casts himself for a role which is unsuited to him and which he is unable to sustain; his ill-fitting "borrowed robes" indicate that he does not possess the histrionic talent of the successful hypocrite. Lear discovers that he had only played at being a king in his royal robes; realizing that they were an obstacle to his comprehension of, and sympathy with, the human condition, he strips off these "lendings" to bring himself to the level of "unaccommodated man." Coriolanus, the proud patrician, is persuaded by his mother to attempt to disguise his true nature beneath the "gown of humility"; he too fails to successfully enact the part. On the other hand, the "shows" arranged by the evil characters are brilliantly effective while they last: "Robes and furr'd gowns hide all."[7] But Shakespeare the dramatist and actor makes it clear that to use the art of playing for concealing reality is totally contrary to its true purpose, which has always been to hold the mirror up to nature. In *Hamlet,* the enactment of "The Murder of Gonzago" achieves the true end of drama--to reveal the truth and not to hide it. The heroes who come after Hamlet share his contempt for the kind of acting which disguises the true nature of human beings. They are isolated because they refuse to accept the dichotomy between appearance and reality that characterizes their social environment.

In the light of this, it is clear that the frequent use of solioquy by the tragic hero is no clumsy stage device. It is the natural corollary of the isolation of the hero, his only medium for expression when dialogue with other characters fails as a means of communication with the audience. Shakespeare is able to exploit the dramatic resources of the soliloquy in his major tragedies because he is writing the kind of drama which is, in the words of Una Ellis-Fermor.

> preoccupied with individuals, which deepens and extends our knowledge of the characters' inner experience not so much by indicating their affinities with a common background of thought and knowledge or with

> a surrounding universe, as by revealing more fully the essence of their individual thought and emotion.[8]

Seen from this point of view, the hero's declaration "I am myself alone" is the appropriate culmination of the tragic process: the hero, who has drawn his breath in pain inthis harsh world, asserts his right to tell his story, to establish his identity. In the major tragedies of Shakespeare, the "total concern for 'self', for identity, is a definding characteristic of the tragic hero."[9] In his ability to project this intense self-consciousness and its complex relationship with social consciousness Shakespeare adds a new dimension to English tragedy. The truly tragic voice is heard when the focus shifts to "a man alone in his extremity,"[10] a situation in which he has no other resources except his own integrity and dignity.

Equipped with these, the hero meets his death with nobility. There is no equivocation, no evasion of responsibility. There is only an attempt, almost choric in character, to place his isolation from his social group in paper perspective. The tragic situation in each case is different, the nature of each hero is different, and if there is any formula which covers the kinds of isolation which Shakespeare's tragic heroes suffer it is, as Douglas Bush has said, "that, in diverse ways and degrees, if only in a momentary flash, they all attain a truer knowledge of themselves and others."[11] In this lies the final value of tragic experience.

Naturally all the heroes do not share an identical mode of awareness, nor is the intensity or breadth of their relationships similar. Hamlet, as the most introspective, is fully aware of the great importance of loyalty in human relationships, but he is not satisfied until he has revealed to the society of Denmark that it is the violation of this loyalty which is at the root of its corruption. Macbeth is the reverse of this. He knows that he will be guilty of the vioolation of the most sacred relationships by committing the murder of Duncan. His imagination is, in fact, able to anticipate vividly the isolation that will ensue if he perpetrates the sacrilegious act, but he makes the tragic mistake of disregarding its warnings. It is only when the mockery of a usurped throne and the treacherous ambiguity of "supernatural soliciting" are revealed to him that he expresses a longing for his lost link with humanity. Lear, the only hero who is a rightfully reigning monarch, is a man of multiple relationships, but acquires awareness of their significance only after deep suffering, the most moving feature of which is his renunciation of all that he had depended upon.

Growth of awareness in the two Roman heroes, Antony and Coriolanus, is depicted somewhat differently. Antony's dilemma is, in a certain sense, the most complex. His social position in Rome is deeply meaningful to him, and he takes great pride in recalling the legendary associations of his family with Roman history. It is not easy for him to sacrifice his membership of the triumvirate to the fascinating but variable relationship with Cleopatra. The peculiar pattern of oscillation that characterizes the play is a result of the difficulty of choosing between public honour and private affection: it is only after the battle of Actium that Antony is forced to acknowledge the supermacy of his love for Cleopatra. Unlike Antony, Coriolanus is not the descendant of a famous Roman family. The imaginative sweep of his world is limited, both in the range of relationships and in self-knowledge, because his undisputed status as a martial leader in Rome blinds him to the deeper levels of his own character. He begins to become aware of these when the issue of the consulship, and the banishment consequent upon it, compel him to realize that personal and social relationships are much more complex than the simple code of a warrior, however honourable it may be. And he pays for this knowledge with his life.

Because they attempt to relate, and not to choose between, self-awareness and social awareness, the heroes of Shakespeare's major tragedies cannot be regarded as the progenitors of the Romantic or modern "alienated" hero.[12] They are obviously modelled on the Renaissance concept of the Great Man—they are courtiers, soldiers, scholars, "Th' observ'd of all observers"—and would normally expect to be at the centre of society rather than withdrawn from it. That situations should arise which compel them to stand outside their world is a *tragic* fact and not simply a statement of the endemic role of such characters vis-a-vis the social group. The focal role of these heroes is indicated by the social consequences of their banishment. Society itself begins to disintegrate—"Things fall apart; the centre cannot hold;"—because the hero is the true centre of his world. In destroying him, society impoverishes itself. Those who remain speak in hushed, reverential voices about the dead because a sense of their own ordinariness in the presence of the heroic overwhelms them: it is a moment of truth for them too. They mourn for themselves as well as for the hero, finally acknowledging that he added a new dimension to their limited awareness. Each hero is a rare spirit who tries tosteer humanity in his direction; inevitably the attempt is resisted, with tragic consequences for the individual and for the community.

Finally, we would like to suggest that it is Shakespeare's unrivalled exploration of this tragic dilemma which has enabled each generation to find contemporary significance in the major tragedies. To a certain extent, each of these plays is not only a tragedy but also a debate,[13] the point at issue remaining eternally unresolved, and therefore, perennially fascinating: what is the extent of social compromise desirable for a socially eminent, socially responsible but personally self-aware individual? Should he assert his identity even at the risk of isolation? As usual, Shakespeare is content to dramatize the problem, leaving us to draw our own conclusions and to make our own choices. In the following chapters an analysis is being made of Shakespeare's presentation of the hero in relation to his social group, with special emphasis upon the dramatic significance of his isolation.

REFERENCES

1. The Jacobean Shakespeare: Some Observations on the Construction of the Tragedies," *Stratfor- upon Avon Stu-ies* I: *Jacobean Theatre* (1960), p. 20.

2. *Shakespearean Trage-y,* 2nd ed. (London, 1905), pp. 19-21.

3. *Hamlet, Father an- Son* (Oxford, 1955), p. 77.

4. *The Story of the Night* (London, 19(1), p. 135.

5. Ibid. p. 136.

6. Douglas Bush, "The Isolation of the Renaissance Hero," in *Reason an- Imagination: Stu-ies in the History of I-eas* 1600-1800, ed. J.A. Mazzeo (London, 1962), p. 57.

7. For a fuller discussion see Anne Righter, *Shakespeare an- the I-ea of the Play,* Penguin ed. (1967), pp. 62-63.

8. "A Technical Problem: The Revelation of Unspoken Thought in Drama," in *The Frontiers of Drama,* University Paperbacks (London, 1964), p. 104.

9. Peter Mercer, "*Othello* and the Form of Heroic Tragedy," *Critical Quarterly,* XI (1969), p. 49.

10. Raymond Williams, *Mo-ern Trage-y* (London, 1966), p. 89.

11. *Op. cit.,* p. 67, G.K. Hunter grants positive value to the isolation of Lear but denies it to that of Macbeth, Antony and Coriolanus. See "The Last Tragic Heroes," *Stratfor- upon Avon Stu-ies* 8: *Later Shakespeare* (1966), esp. pp. 12-14.

12. For a fuller discussion, see Raymond Williams, *op. cit.,* esp. pp. 94, 138.

13. See D.J. Enright, "*Coriolanus*: Tragedy or Debate?", *Essays in Criticism,* IV (1954).

2

Hamlet

The visual presentation of Hamlet's aloofness is more dramatic than that of any other Shakespearean tragic hero. At his first appearance, in Act I sc. ii, he remains defiantly aloof from the business of Claudius' court, though ostensibly he is present to take his allotted share of royal favour. The ingratiating, silken phrases of the new king flow smoothly, but 64 lines of dialogue are spoken before the hero, dressed in his "inky cloak," utters a word. His first soliloquy makes it clear that though he is Prince of Denmark, he is no loyal supporter of the King. This makes a study of Hamlet's isolation particularly complex. Lear makes his first appearance on the stage every inch a king of ancient Britain, Macbeth's entrance is preceded by description of him by a popular king as "valiant cousin! worthy gentleman!" Antony and Coriolanus are unpopular with Romans from the very beginning, but both attempt political compromises which in the event they find impossible to respect. Hamlet, however, comes before us when the schism between him and his environment is already deep; the gulf grows more unbridgeable as the play proceeds. Soliloquy is his characteristic mode of revelation: through it we are given not only his self-analyses but also his reactions to other characters. His frequent soliloquies do underline his isolation, but it is only when we divorce them from their context in the play that we can be misled into thinking of them as indications of "self-centredness"[1] or of "the prevalence of the abstracting and generalizing habit over the practical."[2]

Shakespeare takes special care to emphasize the social awareness of Hamlet, and his full participation in the life of the court before the accession of Claudius to the throne of Denmark. Indeed, we miss one of the most poignant aspects of the tragedy if we underestimate the importance of the carefully placed retrospective references to Hamlet as the complete Renaissance gentleman. More than any other hero, he has been the cynosure of his society, as is indicated by the famous choric description of him by Ophelia:

> The courtier's, soldier's, scholar's, eye, tongue, sword;
> Th' expectancy and rose of the fair state,
> The glass of fashion and the mould of form,
> Th' observ'd of all observers--
>
> (III. i. 151)

The vast range of his thought and experience is reflected in the varied nature of the interests that he displays in the course of the play. He has an almost professional knowledge of dramatics, is conversant with music, and can most delightfully parody the circumlocutory verbiage of the lawyer and the sycophantic courtier. The Prince of Denmark, even more than Prince Hal, is able to attune himself to "all humours that have showed themselves humours since the old days of goodman Adam."[3] It is this well-rounded personality that causes him to be "lov'd of the distracted multitude." The common man of Denmark is ignorant of the change that has taken place in the social position of the Prince; this serves to remind us that the isolation of Hamlet is a recent phenomenon, and only the courtly circle is aware of it.

Even within this narrow circle, the intensity of the cleavage is not apparent until Act II. The spectator or reader, who has been taken into confidence by the first soliloquy of Hamlet, becomes aware of it earlier than any of the characters in the play. Laertes in his advice to Ophelia does not refer to the Prince as an egocentric individualist, but as one who must respect his obligations as a member of the Danish royal family.

> He may not, as unvalued persons do,
> Carve for himself; for on his choice depends
> The sanity and health of this whole state;
> And therefore must his choice be circumscrib'd
> Unto the voice and yielding of that body
> Whereof he is the head.

(I. iii. 19)

When Claudius, in Act I sc. ii, concludes his carefully prepared speech to Hamlet by promising him the place of "chiefest courtier," he is simply offering him his recognized status during his father's reign. And it is exactly this attempt to pretend that nothing has changed which is so abhorrent to Hamlet. While his father—"so excellent a king"--was alive he was proud to be the king's "chiefest courtier" and "son": but to accept that status now in relation to this satyr-like uncle and his incestuous queen! His first solioquy tells us of his disgust with their rank and gross world. He has seen at the meeting of the Council that he is alone in feeling this; Claudius' *fait accompli* has won the support of the other courtiers whose "better wisdoms" have "freely gone/With this affair along." He is doubly isolated; the other characters have neither the absolute moral standards of his idealistic philosophy of human relationships, nor do they feel their flesh "sullied"[4] as he must, because Gertrude is his mother. So his horror of her remarriage must corrode his soul in secret: "But break, my heart, for I must hold my tongue."

His encounter with the spirit of his dead father aggravates the isolation of Hamlet. When the Ghost sees Hamlet waiting with others, it makes a gesture which is precisely interpreted for us by Horatio:

> It beckons you to go away with it,
> As if it some impartment did desire
> To you alone.

(I. iv. 58)

It is a family secret that the Ghost discloses to Hamlet and the mandate is to the son alone. Hence the emphasis on the ritual of making his friends swear "Never to speak of this that you have heard," the thrice reiterated "Swear" of the Ghost running like a refrain, checking any impulse in Hamlet to confide in his friends. It is not his "pride"[5] that makes him falter in trusting his friends; a highly complex combination' of circumstances and Hamlet's own characteristic attitude compel him to be secret and to pursue his mission alone.

Viewed in this light, Hamlet's reaction to the Hecuba speech becomes much more meaningful. What he envies the Player is not the intensity of emotion but the public expression of it. If he could indulge his "passion" of grief for his murdered father openly, he would also

> down the stage with tears,
> And *cleave the general ear* with horrid speech;
> *Make mad the guilty*, and appal the free.
>
> (II. ii. 555)

This is indeed what he attempts to do in the Play Scene and, as has often been remarked, his mode of action undergoes a radical change after this. His public accusation, however oblique, provokes Claudius' open hostility, which culminates in the plan to have Hamlet murdered. Until then, Hamlet

> can say nothing; no, not for a king
> Upon whose property and most dear life
> A damn'd defeat was made.
>
> (II. ii. 563)

His desire to bring Claudius to a public exposure is not the outcome of any legalistic scruple. The command of the Ghost is specific on this point; if he loved his father, he must revenge his "foul and most unnatural murder." The entire emphasis of the Ghost's narrative is on the *personal* crime of Claudius, the single *act* of fratricide, for which the retribution would be a simple "act" of revenge by Hamlet. The Ghost laments the "lust" of Gertrude but makes her guilt passive, so that she is excluded from the revenge. And it is on this point that there is a basic contrast between the attitudes of father and son, in which inheres the essence of the tragedy. The relationship between King Hamlet and Prince Hamlet has been made by Shakespeare a very complex one, in a way hardly hinted at in his sources;[6] as they discuss Hamlet's duty to take revenge, we must understand that each has his own interpretation of the nature of the task. To Hamlet, "my revenge" means something more than the murder of one villain in Denmark. Before he knew of his father's murder, Denmark was to him "an unweeded garden"; what the Ghost tells him does not alter his concept of the society he lives in, it only confirms his prophetic feeling that his uncle is the source of the "rank and gross" corruption that is undermining the state. Apart from the fulfilment of the Ghost's command, there is much that Hamlet has to do to restore "the sanity and health of this whole state."

His personal way of interpreting his task is expressed dramatically in his juxtaposition of Gertrude's and Claudius' guilt after his father's spirit has faded away. To him the horror of his mother's sin is paramount and his comment on her, "O most pernicious woman," is in continuation of the mood of his first soliloquy, rather than in deference to the Ghost's injunction to "leave her to heaven." His next thought is of Claudius, and the incredible hypocrisy of his advances of Hamlet in the Council scene: "O villain, villain, smiling, dammed villain!" He remembers also the obsequious demeanour of the courtiers, and announces to his friends:

> There's never a villain dwelling in all Denmark
> But he's an arrant knave.
>
> (I.v. I23)

Besides the personal sin of Claudius, there is "much offence"; unless he can root out all the corruption that infects Denmark, the private revenge, to his way of thinking, will be pointless.[7] That is why his way of stating his mission is significantly different from that of the Ghost:

> *The time is out of joint.* O cursed spite,
> That ever I was born to set it right!
>
> (I. v. 189)

In interpreting his responsibility in this way, he is not escaping from the particular duty enjoined on him by the Ghost; on the contrary, his moral grasp enables him to relate the personal to the social problem. But, having done that, it is not easy to see where the solution lies. It would be a mistake to think that Hamlet's agonized meditation on the nature of his duty makes his tragedy one of "diseased thought."[8] In his soliloquies, he is not trying to find excuses for delay but is "struggling towards comprehension of what deed is required of him."[9]

Hamlet is alone in trying to resolve this dilemma; he cannot share it even with Horatio. One school of criticism sees Hamlet's problem in terms of excess of "passion"; Horatio, by contrast, is one who is not "passion's slave," and therefore worthy of admiration.[10] This kind of criticism exaggerate the importance of one particular speech, Act III sc. ii 61 ff, and to ignore other parts of the play where this contrast between the two friends is further amplified. Horatio shares with Hamlet an education at Wittenberg, but the difference between the heir to the throne and the withdrawn scholar in illuminating. When Horatio came to Elsinore, he knew of the incestuous royal marriage which had followed hard upon the funeral of Hamlet's father. Yet, among the possibilities to account for the supernatural visitation of the Ghost, he does not include this moral trespass, for it is none to him. On the second appearance of the Ghost, when Hamlet follows it, Horatio is the very soul of discretion and attempts to restrain the rash prince. Horatio's passivity, bordering on indifference, is brought out in his lack of initiative after Hamlet has broken away from his restraining hands. The suggestion to follow him comes from Marcellus, as does the premonition that the Ghost has come to disclose to Hamlet that something is rotten in the state of Denmark. Unlike Hamlet, Horatio is not personally responsible for the state, so he can calmly wait for "Heaven" to "direct it." The pattern of their relationship is the same to the end. Hamlet accepts any challenge to his courage, moral or physical, and courts danger; Horatio is the friend who would restrain him. That is why he is the confidant of Hamlet, but not his partner; the Prince suffers the anguish of decision and action in a complex situation, whereas Horatio remains an impassive stoic. He stands at one remove from experience, one fit to tell the tragic story but not to live it.[11] Hamlet is thus isolated even from Horatio by his "superior power of insight into, and reflection upon, his situation, and his capacity to suffer the moral anguish which moral responsibility brings."[12] Though his conviction falters, and he is overcome by momentary envy of one who "in suff'ring all... suffers nothing," yet his choice, "to take arms against a sea of troubles,/And by opposing end them" is nobler.

And here we are at the core of the tragedy. But the heroic conception of man's duty and destiny Hamlet is involved in a tragic dilemma. It is an aspect of the tragic fact, as presented in this play by Shakespeare, that, if he is to discharge his responsibility, Hamlet's nature must be "subdued to what it works in, like the dyer's hand." He knows not "seems," but the others, inured to hypocrisy, will not accept the surface meaning of his words. So he must put on an "antic disposition"; his feigned madness becomes a vehicle for exposing the truth in a corrupt society which is determined to hide it. He even cultivates a special kind of prose for this role; the main effect of this idiom is "to isolate Hamlet from everyone whose discourse runs in the expected rhythms, so that we are continually and painfully reminded of his exceptional predicament."[13] As he bitterly remarks to Polonius, "to be honest, as this world goes, is to be one man pick'd out of ten thousand." To make the Danish court "honest," he must devise his own methods which cannot be shared with anyone else, since Horatio is too remote from this world, and the others are underlinings of Claudius.

We should not underestimate, in this context, the disillusionment of Hamlet in his relationship with Rosencrantz and Guildenstern. On their first appearance at the court of Elsinore, Claudius refers to them as "being of so young days brought up" with Hamlet, and enlists their help because they are "so neighbour'd to his youth and haviour." Claudius is, if anything, a shrewd man, and the fact that he thinks the two friends have greater access to Hamlet than either he himself or the Queen, makes it obvious that he is not merely indulging in flattery. To them, the mission of spying on their friend seems nothing ignoble; it is easy enough to command them when they have been assured of "such thanks/As fits a king's remembrance." Hamlet, of course, knows nothing of this when they first come to see him; his greeting to them is spontaneous and free from suspicion: "My excellent good friends' How dost thou, Guildenstern? Ah, Rosencrantz! Good lads, how do you both?" He turns to them with obvious relief from his verbal duel with Polonius; they are friends with whom, he hopes, he can share his thoughts on the state of Denmark. There is at first no constraint between them as they indulge in bawdy *camaraderie.* But, though Hamlet is relaxed, they are tense because they are waiting for an opportunity to pluck out the heart of his mystery. Hamlet senses this, and hissuspicions are aroused. Their pretence cannot withstand his incisive questioning; they are compelled to confess that they were sent for. Once they have acknowledged this, he at once changes his manner towards them, from the bluff heartiness of school-fellows to the elaborately formal idiom which later finds its perfection in his dialogue with Osric.[14] Hamlet's anguish at their betrayal is expressed in the way he "conjures" them to be "even and direct" with him, "by the obligation of our ever-preserved love." But, as earlier with Gertrude, so now with them, Hamlet discovers that such obligations have no sanctity in the world reigned over by Claudius. After he has forced Rosencrantz and Guildenstern to confess that they were "sent for" he gives them a description of his state of mind which is *deliberately* exaggerated and generalized, so that it is no more than a philosophical elaboration of the courtly style he has adopted with them.[15] He knows very well why he has lost his mirth, but these erstwhile friends are not to be trusted with the disclosure of the Ghost; that terrible burden makes him a lonelier man as the play proceeds.

Denmark begins to become a "prison" in the literal sense, as the feeling grow in Hamlet that he is under constant watch.[16] What he learns much later than we do is that Ophelia has also been questioned about her relationship with him. Her father is not a man to respect the sanctity of such attachments, so he asks her point blank: "What is between you? Give me up the truth." She seems to have no doubt herself of Hamlet's love for her.

> My lord, he hath importun'd me with love
> In honourable fashion...
> And hath given countenance to his speech, my lord,
> With almost all the holy vows of heaven.
>
> (I. iii. 110)

Her tragedy is that she is not yet mature and independent enough to put loyalty to the man who loves her above obedience to her father. Out of a sense of "duty and obedience" she shows Hamlet's letters to her father; the irony of the situation is obvious when we listen to the one that is read out. Whether we regard it as good poetry or bad, there is no ambiguity in the emphasis of it.

> 'Doubt thou the stars are fire;
> Doubt that the sun doth move;
> Doubt truth to be a liar;
> But never doubt I love.
>
> (II. ii. 115)

In this respect Ophelia has already betrayed him, herself beguided by those who doubt that he loves. In a society in which "drabbing" is part of the accepted way of life of king and courtier it is but natural to assume that the prince is a follower of the fashion.

That Hamlet does not regard the bond between him and Ophelia lighly is clear from the manner in which he appears in her closet after his encounter with the Ghost. The state of shock in which he goes to her is describe graphically by Ophelia:

> Pale as his shirt, his knees knocking each other,
> And with a look so piteous in purport
> *As if he had been loosed out of hell*
> *To speak of horrors*--he comes before me.
>
> (II. i. 81)

Knowing the "hell" he has glimpsed through the hints of the Ghost about the nature of his "prison-house," and the "horror" that he has learnt, of his father's "most unnatural murder," we realize that she speaks truer than she knows. There is litle doubt that when Hamlet falls to such perusal of her face "as 'a would draw it," he is trying to judge whether this young girl whom he loves is capable of sharing his secret.[17] But her face reflects fear alone, the fear with which she rushes to Polonius, crying "O my lord, my lord, I have been so affrighted." So he turns away from her, knowing that a whole world of the experience of evil divides them; in this crisis, she is powerless, because she has no comprehension of the issues at stake. It is this that is implicit in his farewell to her; the poignant acceptance of the fact that she cannot share his burden.

Before he meets her again, in Act III sc. i, the discovery of the spying activities of the courtiers has made him wary and suspicious But his greeting to her, "Nymph, in the orisons/Be all my sins remember'd" shows that he still regards her as innocent.[18] Ophelia's tragedy is played out in this scene; her very innocence makes her a willing decoy in the hands of the unscrupulous Polonius and Claudius, for whom base intrigue is so normal a course that they regard themselves as "lawful espials." The interpretation that can be put on her actions by Hamlet could never have occurred to her when she agreed to let herself be 'used' to test the sentimental theory of her father about Hamlet's madness, Ironically, Polonius had anticipated Hamlet's reaction when he advised his daughter to pretend that she was praying, in order that

> *Show* of such an exercise may colour
> Your loneliness.--We are oft to blame in this:
> 'Tis too much prov'd, that with devotion's visage
> And pious action we do sugar o'er
> The devil himself.
>
> (III. i. 45)

Hamlet has never known "seems" now more than ever he is distrustful of elaborate "shows"[19] because he has learnt that his mother was only a "seeming virtuous queen," his smiling uncle a "damned villain" and his schoolfellows spies.

Had Ophelia been a consummate actress, she would have played her part more skilfully. But being the child she is, she is in a hurry to come to the point--the returning of Hamlet's gifts to him. At once, the incongruity between her pose and the true motive behind it, drives him to the verge of hysteria, and he becomes convinced that she is no better a woman than his mother. That is why his bitterness towards Ophelia anticipates in many respects his triade against Gertrude in Act III sc. iv. In her too there is the dichotomy between appearance and reality, the absence of the kind of loyalty that places trust above any expediency; this makes him feel isolated in the world of false pretence that is Elsinore. His realization of her betrayal is expressed, characteristically, in an abrupt change of idiom and rhythm of speech. As soon as his suspicions are aroused, he confronts her with a direct question: "Ha, ha! Are you honest?" She has no comprehension of his meaning, and her confusion he construes as guilt. He is ashamed of having loved one like her, so he destroys even the memory of their love; "I loved you not."

There is, it appears to Hamlet, nothing untainted; "We

are arrant knaves all; believe none of us." And this is before he realizes that her father is eavesdropping on this ostensibly holy devotion of his daughter.[20] Now he will spare them nothing; his outburst here expresses the frustration of one who finds himself "benetted round with villainies"; it is a world in which none of the fundamental relationships--marriage, love, friendship--seem to have any sanctity. This has made him mad; here his madness is indeed the expression of a deep shock and not a consciously assumed "antic disposition." Realizing how far the corruption emanating from Claudius has blasted the wholesome atmosphere of Denmark, Hamlet decides to strike at the root of the infection. His reckless challenge to Claudius, "I say we will have no more marriage: those that are married already, all but one, shall live;" is the outcome of such a state of mind. Though no clear plan has been formulated, he seems determined to bring Claudius not only to a recognition but also to a public avowal of his guilt; "The Murder of Gonzago" is changing into "The Mouse-trap."

In this scene we are given a clear indication that Claudius has developed some degree of moral awareness. His aside, prompted by Polonius' sentertious remark on the frequent hypocrisy of "devotion's visage":

> O, 'tis too true!
> How smart a lash that speech doth give my *conscience*!
> (III. i. 49)

shows him willing to acknowledge his guilt, at least to himself. This is extremely important if we are to understand his response to the playing of "The Murder of Gonzago." He is no longer the self-assured smiling villain of Act I sc. ii; that is why he breaks down in the way that he does. We sense his discomfort in his reaction to what he has overheard here. He is not sure how much Hamlet knows, but he has begun to panic in his presence.

> There's something in his soul

> O'er which his melancholy sits on brood;
> And I do doubt the hatch and the disclose
> Will be some danger.
>
> (III. i. 164)

He has realized that he had never won "the gentle and unfore'd accord of Hamlet"; he, much more shrewdly than Polonius, has begun to understand the merciless exposure of hypocrisy that Hamlet has been striving at in his "madness." Rather than admit his guilt openly, he seeks to perpetuatge the rottenness of Denmark by exiling Hamlet.

Hamlet, on the other hand, is bent upon breaking through to Claudius' "occulted guilt," normally so well concealed beneath his suave exterior; it is for this purpose that he assumes the role of the chorus when "The Murder of Gonzago" is staged. Suddenly he realizes that unless he insists upon the parallel between the Italian dramatic situation and the Danish actual situation, Claudius would easily be able to pretend that his withers are unwrung. It is his provocative comments, getting nearer and nearer home, which make the King betray his guilt to the more perceptive among the courtiers. It is his final choric flourish, "the talk of the poisoning," that reveals all to, and about, Claudius, and Hamlet is justly proud of it. He has not only got confirmation of the narrative of the Ghost but, even more important, he has succeeded in bringing Claudius to the verge of public acknowledgement of his sin. Once again, two different conceptions of revenge confront Hamlet. He can executive what Bacon called a kind of wild justice and, by killing Claudius, fulfil the command of the Ghost. This might bring private satisfaction but it would in no way lead to the purgation of the state of Denmark; the "imposthume" would inward break and show "no cause without/Why the man dies." On the other hand, he can take the more Christian way and hope to bring the sinner to repentance; this would indeed restore the sanity and health of the state. From the beginning of the play it has been clear that Hamlet's natural inclination is towards the latter alternative, though his love for his father makes him commit himself to the more primitive concept.

This is dramatically highlighted by his sparing Claudius at prayer. Hamlet believes that the revelation of his guilt has made Claudius capable of repentance; he takes his uncle's uncharacteristic posture at prayer to be the first sign that he is getting nearer his objective of setting the time right. And in this general interpretation he is right, even though he is wrong about Claudius' being "fit and season'd for his passage" at this particular moment. To Hamlet this is the most significant kind of revenge, though even now he pays lip-service to the "eye for eye" theory of it propounded by his father's spirit. After the success of the Play Scene he seems briefly possessed by this spirit which prompts him to commit such "bitter business as the day/Would quake to look on." But this is not the true "nature" of Hamlet; it is, as we know, the code of Claudius and, later, of Laertes. Hamlet knows that the use of daggers is much easier, and much less effective, than the exposure of hidden guilt by making the complacent aware of the rottenness that is staining the reputation of Denmark.

Understood in this way, the scene in which he spares Claudius becomes the prelude to Hamlet's interview with his mother. As he had used the Players to "catch the conscience of the King," so with her he will set up a glass where she may see the inmost part of her. At last, he feels, all this secrecy, this spying, is going to end. It is at such a moment that he hears the cry of Polonius; the fury that makes him stab the eavesdropper, believing him to be Claudius, is born of the anguished apprehension that the rottenness is as rank as ever. When he discovers that his attempt at the *act* of revenge has turned out to be a terrible mistake, he turns to his mother to bring her to an acknowledgement that, in marrying Claudius, she had spread the compost on the rank weeds that threaten to choke Denmark. In this he succeeds with her; her moral values have been so limited that she has been genuinely unaware of the monstrousness of her act. It is only now, when she sees it through the eyes of Hamlet, that she realizes the full horror of what she had done; she had betrayed both her first husband and her son. As mother to the Prince of Denmark, she should have matured from the sensuality of her youth, from wife to mother, instead of which she has lived in "the rank sweat of an enseamed bed," false to her husband and to her son. From the beginning of the play it is apparent that Hamlet cannot forgive Gertrude for deserting him and allying herself with Claudius.

Now, some understanding is restored between them as she cried out:

> O Hamlet, speak no more!
> Thou turn'st my eyes into my very soul;
> And there I see such black and grained spots
> As will not leave their tinct.[21]
>
> (III. iv. 88)

It is this "fighting soul" of Gertrude, struggling to "throwaway the worser part" and "live the purer with the other half" which arrests the attention of the Ghost. Though it comes to remind Hamlet of the earlier command, this stern purpose is blunted by compassion for Gertrude; father and son now seem to agree that the sin of Gertrude touches them more deeply than that of Claudius. At last, it seems, Hamlet is free to complete his mission of setting the time right in his own way. When his mother pleads with him, "What shall I do?" there is a fundamental renewal of love between them. From now on she sides with her son rather than with her husband. This is indicated in her attempt to minimize the guilt of Hamlet in killing Polonius and, more significantly, in Claudius explanation to Laertes of his inability to proceed openly against Hamlet: "The Queen his mother/Lives almost by his looks." She keeps her son's secret so well that even Claudius is not shrewd enough to expect her to unmask his treachery in the last scene. He is still politic enough to explain her collapse as a swoon at the sight of blood, but Gertrude redeems herself by exposing his lie to her son:

> No, no, the drink, the drink! O my dear Hamlet!
> The drink, the drink! I am poison'd.
>
> (V. ii, 301)

The scene between Hamlet and Gertrude is the climax of the play; in the course of it Hamlet undergoes a radical change in his attitude towards his appointed task. For one fatal moment he acts like the conventional avenger and commits a "bloody deed"; paradoxically, this futile attempts to obey the command of the Ghsot finally exorcizes this vengeful spirit which has haunted him through the play. As he realizes the implications of the killing of Polonius, he confesses:

> For this same lord
> I do repent; but Heaven hath pleas'd it so,
> To punish me with this, and this with me,
> That I must be their scourge and minister.
>
> (III. iv. 172)

Though, unlike the other characters, Hamlet admits his guilt, the sin lies upon his head; this is how heaven has punished him for putting the dictates of private revenge before the spiritual regeneration which is his duty as heaven's minister. As has often been remarked, except in the "How all occasions inform against me" soliloquy, Hamlet does not again talk in terms of personal revenge; there is a new emphasis on the decrees of "heaven" or "providence." This new confidence is not a form of fatalism; it is the outcome of his feeling that he has set in motion a current of events which will expose the corruption at the court of Denmark, and ultimately destroy it. That is why he can now leave for England without bitter protest; the simple actd of killing Claudius can wait for an opportune moment--"the readiness is all."

Lest we should miss the significance of this change in Hamlet, Shakespeare brings Laertes back to Elsinore, to show the crudity of an avenger who is obsessed with the primitive code of revenge. The contrast between the two sons of murdered fathers is not favourable to the son who rants the louder. He and Claudius, the connoisseur of poison, literally and figuratively, understand each other perfectly; they will use the nobleness of Hamlet against him. Since he has never indulged in the kind of base intrigue that is 'the way of the world' at Claudius' court, he will not suspect in others what he does not know in himself.

> He, being remiss,
> Most generous, and free from all contriving,
> Will not peruse the foils;
>
> (IV. vii. 134)

These two ignoble schemers indeed believe that "revenge should have no bounds," and are certain that Hamlet will not escape a second time. But, after his providential return from the voyage to England, Hamlet is equally certain that with the help of the "divinity that shapes our ends" he will soon succeed in his solitary attempt to restore sanity and health to the state. Rosencrantz and Guildenstern are the first of those, infected by the poison, who are cast out. And the murder of Claudius, now that his regeneration has proved to be impossible--witness his attempt to get Hamlet murdered in England--has acquired a broader significance in his eyes. He asks Horatio:

> And is't not to be damn'd
> To let this canker of our nature come
> In further evil?
>
> (V. ii. 68)

Claudius is the cancerous growth, undermining all life around him, the more vicious for being cloaked beneath a superficial appearance of health.

The last Act very effectively picks up this dichotomy between appearance and reality that Hamlet has been trying to expose single-handed. He has distrusted excessive display of grief ever since he discovered how shallow an emotion underlay his mother's enactment of grief "like Niobe, all tears." As he tells the Players, he recoils from the exaggerated representation of passion: "O, it offends me to the soul to hear a robustious periwigpated fellow tear a passion to tatters." Laertes' theatrical lament at Ophelia's grave provokes Hamlet because he has reason to believe that Laertes' emotion is "in excess of the facts as they appear." This is how he explains his outburst to Horatio; "the bravery of his grief did put me/ Into a tow'ring passion." At first he tries to oppose to it the simplicity and dignity of "This is I,/Hamlet the Dane."[22] With these words he declares himself, ready to accept any responsibility for Ophelia's death that may be laid to his charge. But Laertes is incapable of understanding this; he can only respond in the primitive manner of the conventional figure of revenge. Once again Hamlet loses control as he realizes that, to communicate with others, he must "rant" as much as they. And this time his frustration is the more poignant, because the whole tenor of the burial scene has made him aware that Ophelia had retained her purity and innocence, and that he had condemned her unjustly. In the hyperbole of

> I lov'd Ophelia: forty thousand brothers
> Could not, with all their quantity of love,
> Make up my sum.
>
> (V. i. 263)

he mourns the tragic end to his love, which had become tainted by the suspicion and distrust prevalent at the court of Elsinore. In his attempt to pull out the weeds from the garden of Denmark, he also destroys the flower that was unexpectedly growing among them. He who chooses to bring about a drastic social change, with only his individual judgement to guide him, must accept the inevitable risk of making mistakes, some of which will injure what he holds most dear.

As a foil to his heroic choice, Shakespeare presents in

Ostric the ultimate decadence of the anti-heroic alternative--complete conformity to a corrupt environment. Since the divorce between word and action has been characteristic of the Court of Claudius since the beginning of the play, it is entirely appropriate that its fundamental perversion should find expression in an abuse of language. The "painted word" has become an instrument of concealment and evasion, making communication nearly impossible. It is in connection with the affected style of the grave-diggers that Hamlet first generalizes about the tendency of peasant and courtier to show "slipperiness"[23] in their use of words. The grave-diggers, with their amusing word-play, are no doubt important for providing 'comic relief,' but not as an end in itself. Hamlet takes them light-heartedly, but there is to him something grotesque in their humble imitation of the courtly manner of speech. The smooth style of Claudius is beyond them but their word-play is in direct line of descent from the "foolish figures" of Polonius. There is a mixture of impatience and amusement in Hamlet's remarks to Horatio prompted by his inability to get a straight forward reply to the questions that he asks the grave-diggers:

> We must speak by the card, or equivocation will undo us.
> By the Lord, Horatio, this three years I have took note of it:
> the age is grown so picked that the toe of the peasant comes
> so near the heel of the courtier, he galls his kibe.
>
> (V. i. 133)

As Malone pointed out, "picked" here means "affected"; the nature of the affectation that the peasant is trying to imitate from the courtier is incarnated in Osric. His carefully memorized "golden words" are as false a disguise for his "possession of dirt" as are the "paintings" of a fashionable woman for her real "favour." The fashionable cliche reigns supreme; each courtier has his repertoire of well-worn opinions with which he supports his social role. It is no wonder that Hamlet spurned the place of "chiefest courtier" in such an environment. He is too much in the habit of inquiring into customs and conventions to accept anything at second hand; this inevitably isolates him from the world of Elsinore, of which Osric is a perfect example:

> Thus has he, and many more of the same bevy, that I know the drossy age dotes on, only got the tune of the time and outward habit of encounter--a kind of yesty collection, which carries them through and through the most fann'd and winnowed opinions; and do but blow them to their trial, the bubbles are out.
>
> (V. ii. 183)

Warburton's emendation of the Folio "fond" to "fann'd", accepted by Peter Alexander and many other editors, seems to me to completely distort the meaning of this choric comment by Hamlet. The phrase "fond and winnowed" conveys Hamlet's meaning perfectly; the "opinions" of courtiers like Osric are only "a set of frothy expression suited perpetually to express the absurdest and most over-refined notions."[24] Hamlet's attempt to make Osric speak "in another tongue" exposes the emptiness below the froth; "the bubbles are out." Hamlet has chosen to be bitterly critical of this perversion of the ideal of the courtier, but the tragic burden of opposing a whole world of such men has been a lonely one.

But does Shakespeare show Hamlet critical of the shallowness of the courtly style of Elsinore, only to show him guilty of a more culpable falsehood in his apology to Laertes? To assume this, as has been done by Johnson and others, is to accuse Shakespeare of carelessness at a crucial moment. As Dover Wilson says in his note in the New Cambridge edition: "If there is a suspicion of falsehood or deception, our sympathy with Hamlet (which at this moment of the play Shakespeare is most concerned to enlist) is weakened." If Hamlet is not telling a lie, what do the following words to Laertes mean?

> What I have done
> That might your nature, honour, and exception,

> Roughly awake, I here proclaim was madness.
> Was't Hamlet wrong'd Laertes? Never Hamlet.
> If Hamlet from himself be ta'en away,
> And when he's not himself does wrong Laertes,
> Them Hamlet does it not, Hamlet denies it.
> Who does it, then? His madnes. If't be so,
> Hamlet is of the faction that is wrong'd;
> His madness is poor Hamlet's enemy.
>
> (V. ii. 222)

An unusual stylistic feature of this speech does not seem to have attracted the attention it deserves--the repetition of the name 'Hamlet' seven times through as many lines. What is Hamlet trying to convey through this peculiar play upon his own name? And what is this personified madness which takes Hamlet away from himself and wrong him? In order to answer these questions we must go back to Hamlet's first encounter with the Ghost. When he decides to follow it, Horatio warns Hamlet that the Ghost might "assume some other horrible form" and lead him into madness. And this is exactly what happens, not literally but metaphorically; the Ghost becomes Revenge incarnate-unlike Kyd in *The Spanish Tragedy* Shakespeare coalesces the Ghost and Revenge--and imposes upon Hamlet the role of the traditional avenger. In accepting this role, he determines to wipe away from his memory everything that he had imbibed as the courtier-scholar of Ophelia's description, and become a kind of 'double' of the Ghost, whose commandment shall live all alone in his brain. The vow of vengeance is taken not by Hamlet the Renaissance Prince and Wittenberg scholar but by a man 'possessed' by the spirit of his dead father, also named Hamlet. The 'madness" caused by this is clearly distinguished from the consciously assumed "antic disposition" by the kind of style that is allotted to each; when Hamlet is under the influence of the former, he raves like a bloodthirsty avenger, whereas for the latter he adopts a more sophisticated version of the riddling style of the Food. The former style, which may be called the Ghost's style, is most predominant after the success of the Play Scene when Hamlet's faith in the Ghost is at its peak. The situation is similar to that between Othello and Iago in Act III sc. iii of *Othello*; a noble mind is overthrown and made to lust for blood under the influence of an evil spirit. This is the "madness" that prompts the murder of Polonius, whom Hamlet mistakes for Claudius. This is what Hamlet is trying to say to Laertes--there *is* a Hamlet who has wronged Laertes, not the Hamlet who speaks but his dead father of the same name, whose spirit had tried to impose upon him, contrary to his own nature, the role of the conventional avenger. Hamlet is still too loyal to his dead father to disown his spirit publicly but the hints given in his apology to Laertes are enough to indicate that Hamlet wants to assert, and act according to, his personal values untramelled by the dictates of a primitive code of revenge.

In his last moments, Hamlet is every inch the gracious Prince--courteous, "most generous", an accomplished fencer, fearless in destroying evil and noble in death. Laertes had early said of him, "on his choice depends. The sanity and health of this whole state." Hamlet, to the limit of human endurance, and at the cost of great anguish to himself, has remained faithful to his choice of the means that would enable him to set the time right. He makes some mistakes, and he is brought to the verge of suicide by the complexity and vastness of the task he has undertaken. But at last treachery is locked in and destroyed, even though at the cost of the hero's life, which he had not set at "a pin's fee" from the start. And the sacrifice has not been in vain, because both Gertrude and Laertes die with a new moral awareness, disowning their loyalty to the source of corruption. Claudius, who is unredeemed till the end and whose destruction, therefore, acquires a much wider symbolic significance. Hamlet's obligations towards the state of Denmark continue to be uppermost in his mind; he discharges the last of these by appointing Fortinbras his successor, and deputing Horatio to report his "cause aright."

REFERENCES

1. S. de Madariaga, *On Hamlet* (London, 1948), p. 101.

2. S.T. Coleridge, *Table Talk* (1827), quoted from *Coleridge's Writings on Shakespeare,* ed. T. Hawkes (New York, 1959), p. 139.

3. (*I Henry IV, II,* iv. 89). For the reflection of this in the varied imagery used by Hamlet, see W.H. Clemen, *The Development of Shakespeare's Imagery* (London, 1951), p. 108.

4. I prefer the emendation "sullied," based on the Quartos' "sallied" to the Folio "solid" in Peter Alexander's edition. Perhaps an emendation is not necessary if we accept "sally" as a variant of "sully." See Fredsom Bowers, "Hamlet's Sullied' or 'Solid' Flesh: A Bibliographical Case-History," *Shakespeare Survey* 9 (1956).

5. cf. G.R. Elliott, *Scourage and Minister: a Study of Hamlet* (Duke Univ., Durham, North Carolina, 1951), esp. p. xxxv

6. For a fuller discussion see P. Alexander, *Hamlet, Father and Son.*

7. A subtle theological explanation is necessary to account for this as suggested by Fredson Bowers, "Hamlet as Minister and Scourge," *PMLA* LXX (1955), and much more elaborately, by Eleanor Prosser, *Hamlet and Revenge* (London and California, 1967).

8. D.G. James, *The Dream of Learning* (Oxford, 1951), p. 42.

9. Christopher Fry, "Letters to an Actor Playing Hamlet," *Shakespeare Survey* 5 (1952), p. 61.

10. See L.B. Campbell, *Shakespeare's Heroes: Slaves of Passion* (Cambridge, 1930), p. 147, D.G. James, *op. cit.*, p. 72, and B. Stirling, *Unity in Shakespearian Tragedy* (New York, 1956), p. 74.

11. For a comparison in similar terms, see G.K. Hunter, "The Heroism of Hamlet," *Stranford-upon-Avon Studies 5: Hamlet* (1963), esp. pp. 98-101.

12. Helen Gardner, *The Business of Criticism* (Oxford, 1959), p. 50.

13. Harry, Levin, *The Question of Hamlet* (New York, 1959), p. 117.

14. For the relation of this to "the large topic of social ceremony," see M. Charney, *Style in Hamlet* (Princeton 1969), pp. 173-176.

15. See T. Spencer, *Shakespeare and the Nature of Man* (New York, 1949), p. 94.

16. See R.A. Foakes, "Hamlet and the Court of Elsinore," *Shakespeare Survey 9* (1956).

17. Bradley disagrees; see *Shakespearean Tragedy,* p. 156n.

18. J. Dover Wilson's theory, *What Happen in Hamlet* (Cambridge, 1935), p. 128, that Hamlet had overheard the plan of the "lawful espials" and therefore speaks to her here in a "sardonic tone" seems least convincing on this particular point. See H. Granville-Barker, *Prefaces to Shakespeare: Hamlet,* Illustrated Paperback Edition (London, 1963), Vol. I, p. 286n.

19. For the multiple significance of the word "show" in the play, see Maynard Mack, "The World of Hamlet," *The Yale Review* XLI (1952).

20. The suggestion of Roy Walker, *The Time is Out of Joint* (London, 1948), p. 60, is very apt that it is not by a movement of the arras that Hamlet becomes aware of the eavesdroppers, but by a tell-tale glance of the nervous Ophelia.

21. In view of the clear realization of her sin in these lines, I am unable to understand why Eleanor Prosser, *op. cit.*, p. 1963n, interprets Gertrude's exclamation at line 156, "O Hamlet, thou hast cleft my heart in twain," as an expression of pain at what has happened to her son rather than as a confession of her guilt.

22. Here we agree with H. Granville-Barker, op. cit., p. 163n, that the dignity of this statement is marred if Hamlet leaps into the grave; he must only step forward and declare his presence. Perhaps he should fling aside his "sea-gown" at this point and disclose the Prince dressed in the contemporary royal splendour, not in his inky cloak. Since the others would be dressed in black for the funeral of Ophelia, this would provide a neat antithesis to Hamlet's first appearance.

23. A.P. Rossiter, *Angel with Horns and Other Shakespeare Lectures* (London, 1961), p. 183.

24. Moberly, cited from the new Dover edition (New York, 1963), of H.H. Furness' New Variorum edition, Vol. I.

3

Macbeth

Macbeth resembles Hamlet in that we never see him in a normal relationship with his environment. Lear in that the cleavage between him and society finds overt expression very early in the play. As in Antony's case, the woman he loves impels him to a course of action which isolates him from his social *milieu*. He and Coriolanus are the only two who are condemned as traitors by society; however, whereas Coriolanus is maligned by the plebeians only and has at least the passive sympathy of the nobles, Macbeth's crime leads to his being hounded to death by a whole nation. Moreover, though Coriolanus refuses to return to Rome and is killed by the Volscians, he dies after having acknowledged the supremacy of the ties dictated by Nature; his death is noble because it is the result of his heroic attempt to honour the pledge of a soldier. For Macbeth there is only a barren resolve to fight it out with his opponents:

> Why should I play the Roman fooi, and die
> On mine own sword? Whiles I see lives, the gashes
> Do better upon them
>
> (V. viii. 1)

He is dubbed "tyrant" and "usurper" by his subjects; to the last he is an outcast from the group of which he was once an honoured member. He dies a disillusioned and unloved man even though we, the readers or spectators, know from his agonized soliloquies how acutely he is aware of this and wishes it were otherwise.

Shakespeare gives us hardly any opportunity to see Macbeth mingling with society in a normal fashion. Further, there are no retrospective references to him in the play, such as those which help to give us a balanced view of the characters of heroes like Hamlet and Antony. We are left to deduce for ourselves, from the implications of Macbeth's own words, that his position in society is completely reversed after the murder of Duncan. As the full horror of his crime is revealed to him through the reactions of others, an awareness of his true status as murderer overwhelms him.

> Had I but died an hour before this chance,
> I had liv'd a blessed time; for, from this instant,
> There's nothing serioous in mortality—
> All is but toys; renown and grace is dead;
> The wine of life is drawn, and the mere lees
> Is left this vault to brag of.
>
> (II. iii. 89)

There seems little doubt that here he speaks with perfect sincerity; the words of Malcolm to Macduff, late in the play, bear testimony to this gracious past:

> This tyrant, whose sole name blisters our tongues,
> Was once thought honest; yu have lov'd him well;
>
> (IV. iii. 12)

Even though we have glimpses like these, they are not arresting or frequent enough to be imprinted on the memory. In *Macbeth,* compared to the other tragedies, Shakespeare reduces the number of individualized characters who come in contact with the hero. Duncan and Banquo are two such characters who stand out in the beginning, and Macbeth has been responsible for the murder of both by Act III. Duncan, unaware of the reachery lurking in the mind of his kinsman, commends him as a "valiant cousin" and as a "worthy gentleman." At Forres he expresses his immeasurable gratitude to Macbeth:

Only I have left to say,
More is thy due than more than all can pay.

(I. iv. 20)

After reaching Inverness Duncan speaks with assurance of the "great love" that Macbeth bears to him, and turns to Lady Macbeth saying:

Conduct me to mine host. We love him highly,
And shall continue our graces towards him.

(I, vi. 29)

Duncan trusts Macbeth as kinsman, host, and soldier; no other character in the play voices a similar multiple relationship with the hero. The tragedy lies in Macbeth's desecration of this bond by his murder of Duncan; his isolation is absolute because he violates the deepest personal and political tie.

Macbeth's relationship with Banquo is apparently of a formal nature; they are comrades-at-arms but there does not exist any friendship between them. Even this tenuous relationship is destroyed at their very first appearance. The prophecy of the Witches sows the seeds of rivalry between them, expressed in a brief exchange.

Macb. Your children shall be kings.
Ban. You shall be king.

(I. iii. 86)

Moreover, when Banquo hears Macbeth's reaction to his nomination as Thane of Cawdor, he almost reproves him:

. . . often times to win us to our harm,
The instruments of darkness tell us truths,
Win us with honest trifles, to betray's
In deepest consequence.—

(I, iii. 123)

But "the instruments of darkness" have already begun to lure Macbeth away from the human world; the worst he suspects about what seems to him "supernatural soliciting" is a certain moral ambiguity: it "cannot be good, cannot be ill." His asides in this scene, when he appears "rapt" to the others, anticipate the lack of communication with his fellow beings that is to follow when these secret thoughts are translated into action. He tries to shake off his self-absorbed reverie but his remark to the others, "Let us toward the King," is a kind of Freudian slip, indicative of his desire to rush towards the kingship. His conspiratorial asides to Banquo indicate Macbeth's desire to make him an accomplice in the murder which "yet is but fantastical." Banquo, having no conception of the deed Macbeth is contemplating, readily assents to the suggestion that they speak their free hearts to each other after having considered for some time the strange events of that day.

It is as a natural sequel to this that Banquo again broaches the subject of the prophecies of the Weird Sisters in Act II sc. i. But his casualness becomes tinged with suspicion when Macbeth seems to offer him political bribe:

> If you shall cleave to my consent, when 'tis,
> It shall make honour for you.
>
> (II. i. 25)

Banquo immediately makes his reservations clear; I will consent, he replies, only if I can.

> Still keep
> My bosom franchis'd and allegiance clear,
>
> (II, i. 27)

There is little doubt that Banquo here becomes the spokesman for Macbeth's repressed conscience;[1] Macbeth in his famous soliloquy in Act I sc. vii also acknowledges his obligations towards Duncan, but is persuaded to disregard, them. But Banquo is firm as a rock in his loyalty to the King; when he suspects that Macbeth has violated it, he makes his own stand quite clear:

> Fears and scruples shake us.
> In the great hand of God I stand, and thence

> Against the undivulg'd pretence I fight
> Of treasonous malice.
>
> (II. iii. 128)

The constraint that grows between them after the murder of Duncan is indicated, as always in Shakespeare's major tragedies, by their adoption of an elaborately formal style with each other. Their conversation at the beginning of Act III shows us two hostile persons throwing out diplomatic 'feelers' to each other. Banquo knows that Macbeth played "most foully" to achieve the fulfilment of the prophecies of the "weird women," and Macbeth knows that Banquo may betray him. Macbeth is as panicky about his secret being revealed as Claudius is after the Nunnery Scene in *Hamlet*. It is because of this potential threat, as much as because of the prophecy of the Witches regarding the children of Banquo, that Macbeth decides to kill him. Thus, in the first half of the play, Macbeth destroys the two men with whom he might have had a meaningful personal and political relationship. As a public figure Macbeth is completely without friends; that is why his awareness of the mockery of his titular kingship is so poignantly expressed.

The only deep relationship that Macbeth has is with his wife, his "dearest partner of greatness," though this phrase itself becomes ironical when she ceases to be his partner once the ultimate greatness is achieved. In the larger context of Macbeth's status in society, this particular tie becomes a destructive force, and impels him to the commission of the deed that will isolate both of them. With the valour of her tongue she succeeds in deluding Macbeth into the belief that there is a splendour to be achieved beyond the laws of nature. By equating "th' milk of human kindness" in Macbeth's nature with cowardice, she seeks to make a monster of him. He sees the sophistry of her argument:

> Prithee, peace;
> I dare do all that may become a man;
> *Who dares do more is none.*
>
> (I. vii. 45)

He asserts his bond with the rest of humanity but is persuaded to an unnatural course as he fails to detect the basic fallacy in the argument with which his wife counters his expression of a fundamental human truth.

> What beast was't then
> That made you break this enterprise to me?
> When you durst do it, then you were a man;
> *And to be more than what you were, you would*
> *Be so much more the man.*
>
> (I. vii. 47)

She is here like Milton's Satan encouraging first the angles, and then Eve, to aspire for fulfilment beyond the limits of their hierarchical status. The consequences in all cases are identical: vaulting ambition overleaps itself and "falls on th' other." Instead of the promised ascent to a higher link in the chain of being, there is an irrevocable descent. Lady Macbeth knows this, as the bestiality of her image of herself, dashing out the brains of her own baby, indicates. The tragic impact of this scene is of a most unusual kind; a normal man and a normal woman whipping up their "courage" to pretend too each other that they are capable of the most gruesome brutality! We await the inevitable consequences.

In spite of Lady Macbeth's crucial role in this scene, we must be careful not to exaggerate her influence over her husband. It is important to realize that he never tells her the prophecy of the Witches about the children of Banquo; in his letter to her he reports: "They met *me* in the day of success." As Roy Walker points out, "Lady Macbeth never knows the full reason why her husband is driven to kill Banquo after the first murder has been successfully committed."[2] It is because he does not share this secret with her that she reproaches him:

> How now, my lord! Why do you keep alone,
> Of sorriest fancies your companions making.
>
> (III. ii. 8)

The strain of his lonely guilt brings him to the point of confession:

> O, full of scorpions is my mind, dear wife!
> Thou know'st that Banquo, and his Fleance, lives.
>
> (III. ii. 36)

Her reply, that in them "nature's copy's not eterne," is to her only the statement of a commonplace; to him it is fraught with irony because the prophecy of the Witches seemed to make their copy "eterne" compared to his "barren sceptre." For the second time, he suppresses this from his wife, as he lightly pretends to accept her aphorism as "comfort." He hints at "a deed of dreadful note," and too her query,"What's to be done?" evasively replies:

> Be innocent of the knowledge, dearest chuck,
> Till thou applaud the deed.
>
> (III. ii. 45)

There is a wide gulf between them now; she watches uncomprehendingly as he invokes the powers of darkness:

> Come, seeling night,
> Scarf up the tender eye of pitiful day,
> And with thy bloody and invisible hand
> Cancel and tear to piece that great bond
> Which keeps me pale.
>
> (III. ii. 47)

We must realize that, before he seeks this break with humanity, he has torn to pieces the bond with his wife.

The most dramatic expression of Macbeth's isolation comes in Act III sc. iv, when the Ghost of Banquo appears at the banquet. He is paralysed by fear, oblivious of the assembled guests, and even Lady Macbeth has no inkling of the new horror that is haunting him. She, in her ignorance, chides him for the only one that she knows about:

> This is the very painting of your fear;
> This is the air drawn dagger which you said
> Led you to Duncan.
>
> (III. iv. 61)

Before the banquet he had asked her to give special attention too Banquo, so she has no reason to detect any hypocrisy in Macbeth's repeated references to him. His words to the Ghost seem to her nothing more than the delirium of a guilt-ridden mind tortured by sleeplessness as, we are shown latter, her own mind is. Macbeth, on the other hand, expects the Ghost to be as generally visible as the Witches; his immediate declaration, "Thou canst not say I did it," indicates his desire to believe that there is no reason why the Ghost of Banquo should appear to him alone. At first he thinks that it is her greater self-control that enables her to retain her composure:

> You make me strange
> Even to the disposition that I owe,
> When now I think you can behold such sights
> And keep the natural ruby of your cheeks,
> When mine is blanch'd with fear.
>
> (III. iv. 112)

But slowly it dawns upon him that the terrible "sight" has appeared to him alone. From this point, there is a reversal in their roles: Macbeth not only takes the initiative in evil, he also keeps his crimes secret from his wife. It is long after their commission that she comes to know of the murders that haunt her in her sleep-walking: "The Thane of Fife had a wife; where is she now?... I tell you yet again, Banquo's buried; he cannot come out on's grave." Their marriage is an appearance only; they are in fact not partners in greatness. Her death only completes their alienation from each other; Macbeth reacts to it with weariness because the relationship between them had been destroyed much earlier, leaving each alone in a world of nightmare.

Halfway through the tragedy, Macbeth has been responsible for the murder of his King and of his comrade-at-arms; in committing the second crime he also becomes secretive with the woman who loves him. He is totally isolated, because there is hardly any evidence of love from his other associates. Even before the murder of Duncan, he is more admired as a courageous general than loved as a man; in this respect too he is like Coriolanus. He is presented as winning glory in deeds of violence; a maker of "strange images of death."[3] Such conduct, honourable against enemy forces in wartime, obviously becomes criminal in the normal social context. The tragedy of Macbeth is that the partial fulfilment of the prophecy of the Witches and the eloquence of his wife delude him into believing that manly glory is to be achieved by a murder whose "horrid image" makes his heart knock at his ribs. There is no character like Fortinbras or Cassio to speak an epitaph over him, to recall what he was before tragedy overwhelmed him, but Macbeth himself harks back to a past when he had the normal reactions of a man, before he had become dehumanized by trying to be more than a man:

> The time has been my senses would have cool'd
> To hear a night-shrick, and my fell of hair
> Would at a dismal treatise rouse and stir
> As life were in't.
>
> (V. v. 10)

Throughout the play Macbeth expresses a longing for his lost humanity, but no return to it is possible until he has disavowed his faith in the powers of darkness. He desires to mingle with society and play the humble host but, after the sacrilege that he has committed against the laws of hospitality, this is an impossible wish. Because of his violation of the most sanctified social conventions, he comes to be regarded as a curse on society, and his subjects pray for the day when

> we may again
> Give to our tables meat, sleep to our nights,
> Free from our feasts and banquets bloody knives,
>
> (III. vi. 33)

There is deep tragic irony here; this is exactly what Macbeth, himself denied sleep--"Chief nourisher in life's feast"--longs for, but his conception of the role for which he has been cast by supernatural powers carries him further into his lonely world of crime.

The other characters in the play judge Macbeth by his actions; his thoughts, as I have discussed above, are never fully shared with any of them. They do not know what agony he undergoes, nor the self-torture that finds expression in his soliloquies. No condemnation of his deeds could be more powerful than hiw own:[4]

> ...pity, like a naked new-born babe,
> Striding the blast, or heaven's cherubin hors'd
> Upon the sightless couriers of the air,
> Shall blow the horrid deed in every eye,
> That tears shall drown the wind.
>
> (I. vii. 21)

He realizes the isolation that will ensue, and his fears are neither of the world to come, nor of detection; as Helen Gardner has said:

> It is the judgement of the human heart that Macbeth fears here, and the punishment that the speech foreshadows is ... that having murdered his own humanity he will enter into a world of appalling loneliness, of meaningless activity, unloved himself, and unable to love.[5]

It is this which unnerves him, and prompts the last attempt to withdraw from the murder. He is aware that, if he tries to misappropriate the royal robes, he will forfeit the right even to the

> Golden opinions from all sorts of people,
> Which would be worn now in their newest gloss,
> Not cast aside so soon.
>
> (I. vii. 33)

It is clear that he has no hope of deceiving himself or others about the nature of the act. His awareness of the fate that will follow the regicide is implicit in his solioquy at the beginning of Act II, in which he identifies himself with other outcasts from society. Lady Macbeth may be deluded enough to speak of the murder as "great business" but Macbeth from the first regards it as an act so horrible, so contrary to accepted values, that even the contemplation of it induces a kind of neurosis, a "raptness" in which he loses contact with those around him.[6]

Such unnaturalness, being absent while present, has its counterpart in Lady Macbeth's sleep-walking; she suffers the contradiction of being awake while asleep. These states of mind symbolize their dissociation from normal life, epitomized in Macbeth's negation of natural order--"Nothing is but what is not." The most tragic expression of this elemental perversion is in the hypocrisy that Macbeth adopts, and since "There's no art/To find the mind's construction in the face," he can pretend to be a loyal subject of Duncan even after he has entertained the thought of regicide. There is to be no correspondence between the face and the heart:

> Away, and mock the time with fairest show;
> False face must hide what the false heart doth know.
>
> (I. vii. 81)

From this, it is clear that even for most of the time that we see Macbeth mingling with other characters, he does not really communicate with them; what he presents to them is a mask. In conjunction with the imagery of borrowed robes that runs through the play[7], this dissociation between thought and act looks forward to the actor image in *Coriolanus*. Whereas the Roman asserts his proud nobility by publicly declaring that he is only playing a part in his "gown of humility," Macbeth appears ignoble and unnatural in trying to appropriate the royal robe, no more than a "dwarfish thief." The role that he aspires to is condemned as a reversal of "degree," and

> the heavens, as troubled with man's act,
> Threatens his bloody stage.
>
> (II. iv. 5)

Coriolanus would only wear the vesture of humility and not be humble; Macbeth attempts a dissociation which is fundamentally impossible in the nature of things. He would commit the deed but shut his eyes and his mind to it;[8] he stands with his "hangman's hands" and yet wonders: "But wherefore could not I pronounce 'Amen'?" He wants to disown his bloody hands like an actor returning to the green-room after enacting a murder on the stage: "A little water clears us of this deed./ How easy is it then!" But the hands will not be disowned; though the eyes try to turn away from them, they demand acknowledgement and recognition. All the world may be a stage and the men and women merely players, but the difference is that the roles chosen here have to be adopted for a lifetime. And Macbeth has made the tragic mistake of casting himself for a part which is totally contrary to his true nature; that is why he is unable to sustain it. In his realization of this lies his redemption as a tragic hero; he has made of his life.

> but a walking shadow, a poor player,
> That struts and frets his hour upon the stage,
> And then is heard no more; it is a tale
> Told by an idiot, full of sound and fury,
> Signifying nothing.
>
> (V. v. 24)

A conventional image is used very unconventionally, as John Lawlor has observed:

> The central isolation of Macbeth, prompted and rehearsed in his part and launched upon his career by Lady Macbeth, seems to have touched off in Shakespeare's deepest imagination the central isolation of the actor, alone against a potentially dangerous world of observers, with his brief span of time in which to succeed or fail, and the actor's sharp awareness, spectator-fashion, of the limitations of his art.[9]

When Macbeth realizes the full significance of Duncan's

murder, he formally casts himself for the role of murderer in the life of play-acting to which he has condemned himself: "There's nothing serious in mortality--/All is but toys." Like Othello's murder of Desdemona, Macbeth's murder of Duncan is also a kind of suicide; in each case the tragedy lies as much in the violation of the hero's own nature as it does in the violation of an innocent life. Macbeth "has performed the murder of Renown and Grace for his world, *as well as for himself.*"[10] And, having killed his true self, he is left with nothing but the counterfeit; he stalks through Scotland like his own ghost. He is set apart from the normal world by his numerous experiences of supernatural phenomena. Macbeth's alienation from the world of the living finds its most dramatic expression in the appearance of the Ghost of Banquo; he is condemned in this world--"but here"--as well as in the "life to come." This had been anticipated in Macduff's outcry after the discovery of the murder of Duncan.

> Malcolm! Banquo!
> As from your graves rise up and walk like sprites
> To countenance this horror!
>
> (II. iii. 76)

What Macbeth wished for figuratively is granted to him literally:

> Better be with the dead,
> Whom we, to gain our peace, have sent to peace,
> Than on the torture of the mind to lie
> In restless ecstasy.
>
> (III. ii. 19)

Now he *is* with the dead; his unnatural desire to be superhuman render him inhuman.

As the play proceeds, Macbeth progressively loses touch with the world of reality, and puts complete trust in a world of unreality, where not even his wife can follow him. In *Hamlet* also the Ghost plays an important part, but only in so far as it confirms what Hamlet had already suspected.

Hamlet, at its first visitation, seems to surrender himself completely to the command of his dead father's spirit but, he has his own characteristic way of interpreting his duty. The connection between Macbeth and the Witches is much more ominous, and it is established in the opening scene when they announce their plan to meet Macbeth on the heath. As soon as he and Banquo see them, the latter at once identifies them as "the instruments of darkness." Their appearance is so completely in conformity with the traditional notion of witches that there is no room for the kind of doubt that plagues Hamlet about the nature of the Ghost; these *are* unambiguously agents of the devil. Yet, because they prophesy that he shall be King, Macbeth accepts them as omniscient divine powers. "I have learn'd by the perfect'st report they have more in them than mortal knowledge." Since the curtainraiser is so successful, he is willing to let them direct the drama of his life:

> Two truths are told,
> As happy prologues to the swelling act
> Of the imperial theme.
>
> (I. iii. 127)

When he finds that society does not applaud his role, he seeks out the Witches like a disappointed actor demanding improved direction. But Hecate uses the glory of her art to raise

> such artificial sprites
> As, by the strength of their illusion,
> Shall draw him on to his confusion.
>
> (III. v. 27)

Instead of showing him how he can successfully retain the kingly role, the Witches reduce Macbeth to a spectator: the series of Apparitions, the last of which is "A Show of eight Kings," makes it clear that his enactment of the imperial theme is drawing to a close whereas that of Banquo's posterity extends to infinity. And it seems that the Witches are in a hurry to make Macbeth quit the imperial stage because their ridding answers to his desperate questions set him firmly on the path of self-destruction. By warning him about Macduff and by giving him illusory security from harm by any man "of woman born," they deliberately confound him. Macbeth seems to realize this and cries out:

> Infected be the air whereon they ride;
> And damn'd all those that trust them!
>
> (IV. i. 138)

For a moment it appears that he is going to disown them and return to the world of human reality, but no such thing is possible. The moment he sees the blood of Duncan on his hands, he knows that his violation of sanctified social conventions has been so fundamental that, in the human world, he will always bear the "Ishmael stamp of outlawry"[11] and be a pariah from the ways of men. On *this* store of the sea of blood into which he has waded there is no hope of any return to a sense of community; on the *other* shore there is the hope that he may, at last, "laugh to scorn/The pow'r of man." But we know that, being a man, Macbeth cannot escape the logic of his own humanity, against which he has been struggling since the beginning of the play.

At the end, when Birnam Wood appears indeed to have come to Dunsinane, Macbeth begins to doubt "th' equivocation of the fiend/ That lies like truth"; ironically, this description applies to him as well as to the Witches. With this realization, he begins to win back something of his dignity.[12]

> I gin to be aweary of the sun,
> And wish th' estate o' th' world were now undone.
> Ring the alarum bell. Blow wind, come wrack;
> At least we'll die with harness on our back.
>
> (V. v. 49)

Now there is none of the hypocrisy, the equivocation, that had been a barrier between him and the other characters. He openly confesses to Macduff: "my soul is too much charg'd/

With blood of thine already." With him, he does not find refuge in the alibi that he had offered to the Ghost of Banquo: "Thou canst not say I did it." Finally he acknowledges that, in the world of human ethics, act and desire are inseparable; the sin of the hand must be recognized, whether it is the hand that wields the weapon or the hand that signs the death warrant. The sleepless Macbeth realizes this much more fully than the sleepless Henry IV. And in this lies his claim to tragic stature.

There is only a glimmer of recognition by the other characters of this change in Macbeth. Act V sc. ii has a distinctly choric character; Menteith Caithness, Angus and Lennox give us the general estimate of Macbeth:

> Now does he feel
> His secret murders sticking on his hands;
> Now minutely revolts upbraid his faith-breach;
> Those he commands move only in command,
> Nothing in love.
>
> (V. ii. 16)

He is no Antony to command the loyalty of his soldiers in his moments of failure: "none serve with him but constrained things." We, the readers or spectators, know the anguish the awareness of his isolation brings Macbeth, for we can listen to his lament for his desolate state:

> I have liv'd long enough, My way of life
> Is fall'n into the sear, the yellow leaf;
> And that which should accompany old age,
> As honour, love, obedience troops of friends,
> I must not look to have;
>
> (V. iii. 22)

He has suppressed such thoughts in himself for a long time; now that he gives expression to them it is too late. The several short scenes in the last Act, with various characters echoing each other in their desire for revenge upon him, emphasize his loneliness. They do not know that Macbeth too is weary of being a tyrant, and that their desire—"Meet we the med'cine of the sickly weal"—is fully shared by him, as indicated by his words to the Doctor:

> If thou couldst, doctor, cast
> The water of my land, find her disease,
> And purge it to a sound and pristine health,
> I would applaud thee to the very echo,
>
> (V. iii. 50)

Macbeth is tired of being the "poor player" whose only role has turned out to be that of blood-stained murderer; he would himself now like to watch a change of scene, from sickness to health, from darkness to light. But he himself is the disease biasting his country; his tragedy in this respect is like that of Oedipus. He would not be so, he disavows his faith in the powers of darkness and destruction, but his violation of life has been too absolute for any reconciliation with society to be possible at the end. Hamlet asks forgiveness of Laertes inthe presence of the Court, avenges the deaths of his father and mother, and fulfils his duties as Prince of Denmark before he dies. Lear is reconciled to Cordelia, and is offered the throne by Albany. For Macbeth there are only "curses not loud but deep," from the membres of the society that he has desecrated. There is no epitaph for him other than that of "dead butcher"; he asks for no public forgiveness, no acceptance by society, and none is granted to him. But Shakespeare has seen to it that the social judgement, though perfectly valid, should not be the chief focus of dramatic interest in this play; what he picks out for our attention is the anguish of a man trying to destroy his own humanity and, having done that, longing to break out of the solitary confinement to which he has condemned himself.

REFERENCES

1. See A. Quiller-Couch, *Shakespeare's Workmanship* (Cambridge, 1947), p. 47, and L. Kirschbaum, "Banquo and Edgar: Character or Function?", *Essays in Criticism,* VII (1957), p. 7.
2. *The Time is Free* (London, 1949), p. 43.
3. See John Holloway, *The Story of the Night,* pp. 58-59.
4. As was noted by Bradley, *Shakespearean Tragedy,* pp. 355-356.
5. *The Business of Criticism,* p. 61.
6. See B. Stirling, *Unity in Shakespearean Tragedy,* chapter on *Macbeth* entitled 'Look, how our partner's rapt.'
7. See C. Spurgeon, *Shakespeare's Imagery* (Cambridge, 1935), pp. 324-327, and Cleanth Brooks, "The Naked Babe and the Cloak of Manliness," in *The Well Wrought Urn* (New York, 1947).
8. See K. Muir, New Arden edition (London, 1953), pp. xxxi-xxxii.
9. *The Tragic Sense in Shakespeare* (London, 1960), p. 142. See also V.Y. Kantak, "An Approach to Shakespearean Tragedy: The 'Actor' Image in *Macbeth,*" *Shakespeare Survey,* 16 (1963) esp. p. 49.
10. Wilbur Sanders, *The Dramatist and the Received Idea: Studies in the Plays of Marlowe and Shakespeare* (Cambridge, 1968), p. 257; (emphasis added)
11. G. Wilson Knight, *The Wheel of Fire* (London, 1949), p. 126.
12. We agree with Bradley, *Shakespearean Tragedy,* p. 356, that "in the very depths a gleam of his native love of goodness, and with it a touch of tragic grandeur, rests upon him." I do not find A.P. Rossiter's rejection of this view, *Angel with Horns,* p. 229, in favour of his own, that Macbeth "dies less as a demi-goop than as a gangster," convincing.

4

King Lear

Lear is unique among the heroes of Shakespeare's major tragedies in that he is the reigning monarch when the play opens. He is thus a man of multiple relationships of long standing, which Kent summarises in the following lines:

> Royal Lear,
> Whom I have ever honour'd as my king,
> Lov'd as my father, as my master follow'd,
> As my great patron thought on in my prayers--
>
> (I. i. 138)

Such relationships are not, of course, absent from the other tragedies, but they are not presented with the same dramatic emphasis that they are given in *King Lear*. In *Hamlet* we hear of these relationships from the ghost of the dead King of Denmark, after they have been desecrated by Gertrude and Claudius, or in the bitter comment by Hamlet on the inconstancy of his father's subjects. In *Macbeth* we hear of them very briefly from Duncan with respect to the treachery of Cawdor, or in the imaginative formulation of the obligations towards a king by Macbeth as he contemplates regicide. In neither play is the wronged king the dominating figure, nor is the dramatic impact made through his response to the violation of the traditional loyalty due to a king.

This fact is related to another significant feature of *King Lear*: a synthesis of the public and personal roles of the hero.

Hamlet sets himself the task of setting right something rotten in the state of Denmark but he has to pursue it in complete secrecy, to which he is repeatedly sworn by his father's spirit. The public functions that Macbeth presides at as King are of interest as showing, ironically, his inability to sustain the royal role and his lapse into his private world of "horrible imaginings." In its coalescence of public and personal issues *King Lear* looks forward to the Roman tragedies. As in *Coriolanus* and *Antony and Cleopatra,* the step which ultimately leads to the isolation of the hero is taken in the presence of others. The division of the kingdom by Lear is announced when the entire Court is assembled. This means that the other characters in the play are from the start aware of the situation of the King and, beginning with the remonstrance by Kent, efforts are made to make him realize the implications of his conditional abdication, and to bring about a reconciliation between him and Cordelia. Lear and Antony are heroes of very different qualities, but they have in common a capacity to inspire loyalty in adversity, and they are never as completely alone as are heroes like Macbeth and Coriolanus.

In *King Lear* there is a special reason for this; the pattern of the tragedy emphasizes that the fate of Lear is not unique, at least not in kind, though it is in degree of intensity. To speak of the theme of the relationship between Gloucester and his sons as the 'sub-plot' is to distort the meaning of the tragedy. Shakespeare did not make this addition to the Lear legend to provide variety of episode; the story of Gloucester's family is as closely related to the main theme as are the affairs of the Polonius family to those of the House of Hamlet. The grouping of characters is not according to the part they play in major and subsidiary plots; the antithesis is between two different concepts of human relationships. Bradley comments on this "unusual circumstance" in great detail. If we set apart Lear, Gloucester, and Albany, he points out.

> the rest fall into two distinct groups, which are strongly, even violently, contrasted: Cordelia, Kent, Edgar, the

> Fool on one side, Goneril, Regan, Edmund, Cornwall, Oswald on the others. These characters are in various degrees individualised, most of them completely so; but still in each group there is a quality common to all the members, or one spirit breathing through them all. Here we have unselfish and devoted love, there hard self-seeking.[1]

In the beginning Lear assumes that he can demand love because he combines in himself three attributes to which devotion is due: fatherhood, kingship, and old age. His spiritual development correspondingly falls into three distinct stages. The first shock comes to him when he believes that he has been slighted as a father by Cordelia. As he banishes her, he tries to exact from his other two daughters the deference due to him as King by insisting on keeping his train of knights. His disillusionment comes when he finds Cornwall and Regan unapologetic about their insult to him in the stocking of Kent. When he sends for them he still takes for granted the respect due to him as King and father:

> The King would speak with Cornwall; the dear father
> Would with his daughter speak; commands their service.
>
> (II. iv. 99)

But as soon as the complicity between Goneril and Regan is revealed to him, he turns away from humanity to the gods, pleading for their sympathy merely as

> a poor old man,
> As full of grief as age; wretched in both.
>
> (II. iv. 271)

Regan's reiterated "Shut up your doors" is charged with a special significance: she and her world cast out Lear, denying him the most elementary human compassion. Unable to bear this shock, he withdraws into the world of him own imagination.

In his madness, Lear almost forgets the privileges of

kingship; what is indelibly impressed on his consciousness is the ingratitude of his daughters. Johnson is right in his emphasis on the most moving feature of the tragedy: "*Lear* would move our compassion but little, did we not rather consider the injured father than the degraded king."[2] It is in this context that the primitive setting of the tragedy becomes specially meaningful. In localizing so much of the action of the play on a tempestuous heath, Shakespeare strips Lear's spiritual development of any touch of sophistication. The brittle edifice of deceptive appearances topples down, and Lear has to start building his world of values from the scratch. By his isolation from all that he had depended upon, he is driven to ask "the questions of a Prometheus."[3] Lear's question to Goneril, "Are you our daughter?" is not prompted by any petty sarcasm; it is the starting point of his quest into the validity of human relationships. In the context of this quest, the bond of sympathy among human beings is taken to be fundamental and instinctive; a denial of it is a violation of that one touch of nature which makes the whole world kin. "Unkindness" in this tragedy is to be understood in this elemental sense, and it "spreads through *King Lear* like the poison through Denmark."[4]

In his effort to expose the hypocrisy of the Danish court, Hamlet has two advantages over Lear; his youth and his philosophical discipline as a scholar from Wittenberg. In one way, this isolates Hamlet completely from the other characters; at the same time, his grasp of abstract ideas gives him an inner strength that Lear does not posses. Lear is not set apart from the other characters by the nature of his metaphysical speculations, as Hamlet is. What elevates him to his Titan-like heroic stature is his courage in embarking upon his metaphysical quest, in order to reach himself to distinguish between appearance and reality. What makes his quest so poignant, so basic and child like, is that he is "fourscore and upward." In the light of his later experiences, his announcement of his abdication becomes charged with the profoundest irony:

> ...'tis our fast intent
> To shake all cares and business from our age,
> Conferring them on younger strengths, while we
> *Unburden'd* crawl toward death.
>
> (I. i. 37)

He is compelled to shed more than he had intended to; he is stripped to his bare humanity, and it is only then, from cruel experience at first hand, that he matures to a wider sympathy with wretched and suffering houseless poverty. Lear does not develop spiritual understanding through successive stages of an abstract process; his growth is the result of his progressive isolation from all that he had ever valued and understood. As all familiar supports are withdrawn, he is compelled to an understanding of himself and of the fundamental questions of life, which is deeper than any that ahe had possessed before.

At the start Lear has an obstinacy that he mistakes for virtue. Kent, who has a true understanding of allegiance, tries to intervence on Cordelia's behalf when her father banishes her. But Lear is blind to his error, and declares:

> That thou hast sought to make us break our vows--
> Which we durst never yet--and with strain'd pride
> To come betwixt our sentence and our power--
> Which nor our nature nor our place can bear;
> Our potency made good, take thy reward.
>
> (I. i. 168)

He has already accused Cordelia of pride; Shakespeare leaves us in no doubt about Lear's obsession with his own privileges, which makes him construe as "strain'd pride" anything that does not fall into the familiar rhythem of the idiom of courtly lattery. He is early started on his path of enlightenment. As the ingratitude of Goneril is revealed to him, he becomes aware for what a small fault he had disowned the daughter dearest to him. But this realization brings him no immediate relief, nor a facile reconciliation with Cordelia. That is not to be granted to him until he has been brought, through ultimate deprivation and madness, to a recognition of his deep bond with humanity in general, and with Cordelia in particular. His reunion with Cordelia is not merely the resumption of a relattionship that had existed before and had been temporarily violated; all his suffering and loneliness contribute directly to making the love between them richer and deeper. We have an analogous feeling about the relationship between Coriolanus and Volumnia. In both tragedies, the filial relationship is comprehended in its depth only after isolation has compelled a basic reappraisal of it, though the relationship is examined much more extensively in *King Lear* than it is in the Roman tragedy.

Within such an emotional context, the 'happy ending' so considerately added by the tender-hearted editors of Shakespeare in the eighteenth century, is bound to appear incongruous and anti-climatic. The breach between Lear, the King, and his immediate courtiers is too deep to be ever healed. Before he dies, he has become aware of the love and forgiveness of Cordelia, but he has no recognition of any of the others. Hamlet dies discharging his responsibilities as the heir-apparent to the throne of Denmark, but Lear at the end has completely for all awareness of himself as a monarch; he hardly knows Kent, Albany, and Edgar, and the offer of the throne is meaningless to him. This is made more poignant by the fact that, of all Shakespeare's major tragic heroes, Lear has the most loyal followers: Kent and Edgar are by his side when he is cast out into the storm but, since they are in disguise, he is ignorant of this. All through the play, the reader or the spectator is much more aware of the love and loyalty that surround Lear than he is himself. Until he finds Cordelia, he considers himself forsaken by humanity and, though attempts are continually made to prove the contrary, he dies with no faith in anyone except Cordelia. His reconciliation is intense and satisfying for him but it des not have a wide range.

The importance of Cordelia as a character in the play is much greater than the duration of her actual presence on the stage might indicate. By her conduct in the first scene she becomes "a tragic actor... and not merely a pathetic victim."[5] Shakespeare is able to effect this transformation by the changes that he makes in her characterization in comparison with what he found in the sources of the story. Her inability to express her feelings when questioned by her father in the love-test was part of the legend, but her two asides represent Shakespeare's original contribution.[6] He sets her apart, and through her asides prepares us for her response to the impossible situation Lear is creating for her. She, at this point, should make as powerful a dramatic impact as Hamlet does standing aloof from the smooth flatteries of Claudius' court. As she listens to the "glib and only art" with which Goneril makes her exaggerated protestations of love, she realizes that her nature will not allow her to compete in this test of flattery: "Who shall Cordelia speak? Love, and be silent." She feels a fatal inevitability about the hurt she is going to cause the father she deeply loves as Regan overtops the smooth hypocrisy of Lear's eldest-born:

> Then poor Cordelia!
> And yet not so; since I am sure my love's
> More ponderous than my tongue.
>
> (I. i. 75)

Her difficulty is not limited to her being asked to make a public statement of a deeply personal emotion; she is to make her declaration of love in expectation of a material reward. It is ironical that whereas Goneril and Regan go through their recitation of hypocrisies without their father making an explicit references to the purpose of the love-test, as he turns to Cordelia he unequivocally links her avowal of love to her share of the kingdom:

> ...what can you say to draw
> A third more opulent than your sisters? Speak.
>
> (I. i. 84)

How is she to answers him? To win an opulent share of the kingdom, she can indeed say nothing. Her tragedy is that she has no means of indicating to her father that it is his misguided manner of correlating love and political gain that compels her, if she is to be "true," to give him her desperately bare reply in her embarrassment. Cordelia's sincerity is as much misinterpreted by her father as Coriolanus' is by his mother. There is a close parallel in this respect between *King Lear* Act I sc. i. 81 ff. and *Coriolanus* Act III sc. ii. 28 ff., especially between Lear's words to Cordelia:

> Mend your speech a little,
> Lest you may mar your fortunes.

and Volumnia's more explicit:

> I would dissemble with my nature where
> My fortunes and my friends at stake require'd
> I should do so in honour.

Volumnia tries to persuade her son to indulge in hypocrisy for the reward of the consulship, and in a politic speech pleads with him to recant what he has spoken to the Tribunes. Similarly, Lear in his peremptory "Speak again" is, by implication, tryuing to exact from Cordelia such a hypocritical avowal as has secured shares of the kingdom for her sisters. Both parents show a tragic failure to understand the nobility intheir children which prevents them from yielding to their appeals. In this respect Cordelia belongs to the same class of characters as heroes like Coriolanus and Hamlet: her "calm and steadfast isolation among the contending or subservient figure"[7] makes such a powerful impression in the first scene that her absence from the play for almost three Acts does not erase it.

In addition to this, there is another reason why Cordelia is not forgotten by us: Kent keeps in touch with her, and on her behalf initiates the movement to restore Lear to a more natural world than that of Goneril and Regan. Kent is the first to intercede on Cordelia's behalf, because his code of ethics is the same as hers, and he therefore understands her "plainness" which her father misunderstands as "pride." Cordelia expresses her love for her father in two significant asides, but Kent makes the most comprehensive declaration of loyalty to Lear, in spite of being compelled to chide him in public for his folly. This violation of "hierarchical propriety"[8] causes as much pain to Kent as Cordelia's "Nothing" does to her, because his devotion is as sincere as her love. His love is as incapable of being destroyed by injury as hers is; when he reappears, disguised, in Act I sc. iv, to offer Lear his service, he expresses his loyalty in terms very similar to those he had used before being unceremoniously banished by his master: "you have that in your counternance which I would fain call master," which is "Authority." And he is true to his word; he follows his "enemy king" and does him service "improper for a slave." His devotion is as embarrassed by reward as Cordelia's love is: "To be acknowledg'd... is o'erpaid." The most poignant moment in Kent's relationship with Lear comes in the last scene; he tries to make his master recognize him, to be "acknowledg'd," only to alleviate Lear's desolation when he enters with Cordelia dead in his arm. As he perceives a faint glimmer of recognition in the old eyes, he encourage Lear to remember him. He is the same man, he assures him,

> That from your first of difference and decay
> Have follow'd your sad steps.
>
> (V. iii. 288)

But it is in vain indeed; Kent's service is not to end in this world. He has no place in the new world of Albany and Edgar; he is separated from them by a whole generation. His only ambition is to follow Lear: "My master calls me; I must not say no".

Kent and Cordelia represent a world of values in which Lear is provileged as King, as father, and as an old man. It is the reverence due to all these that constitutes the "Authority" the Kent wants to serve. In banishing him Lear places himself in a world where "the ideal of service is overthrown, and the spirit of *time*-serving usurps the kingdom."[9] When Lear makes the stipulation on dividing the kingdom between Goneril and Regan, that he will retain a hundred knights, and the name "and all th' addition to a king," he has no idea that by giving up his political power, he has placed himself at the mercy of those who understand no ethics except those of self-interest. As R.B. Heilman has pointed out,[10] there are two views of age represented in the play. According to one view, held by Lear and Gloucester as old men, and by Cordelia and Edgar as children, old age is allied with nature, its special due being respect and kindness. The other view is represented by Goneril's equation of old age with dotage; she sees only foolishness in Lear's claim to any kingly "addition" once he has announced his abdication:

> Idle old man,
> That still would manage those authorities
> That he hath given away! Now, by my life,
> Old fools are babes again, and must be us'd
> With checks as flatteries, when they are seen abus'd.
>
> (I. iii. 17)

This is spoken not to her sister, but to Oswald, and is in continuation of her advice to him and the other members of her household to put on "what weary negligence" they please. Men like him know no principle except that of falling in with the mood of whoever happens to be in power; it is appropriate that he and his kind are thus described by Kent, who stands for values which are diamentrically opposed to those of time-serving:

> Such smiling rogues as these,
> Like rats, oft bite the holy cords a-twain
> Which are too intrinse t' unloose;
>
> (II. ii. 68)

That is the tragedy; people of this kind, who recognize no bond as holy, yet have the power to bring about the isolation of those who find life meaningless when divorced from fundamental human ties. Kent himself had defined his master when he saw him being taken in by flattery, but Oswald and time-servers like him

> Renege, affirm, and turn their halcyon beaks
> With every gale and vary of their masters,
> Knowing nought, like dogs, but following.
>
> (II. ii. 73)

It is to them, and not to all his subjects, that Lear's bitter words in Act IV sc. vi apply: to them "the great image of authority" does not inhere in the personality of an old king, as it does for Kent. Men like Oswald are the perfect followers for Goneril because to her too Lear's hope of retaining the name and status of a king after relinquishing the office seems mere fatuity.

Lear notices "a most faint neglect" on the part of Goneril and her followers but tries to avoid interpreting it as "a very pretence and purpose of unkindness." It is significant that he asks for the Fool at this point. If Lear is unwilling to recognize Goneril's unkindness for what it is, the Fool will leave him under no illusion. The Fool is a character with a dual function. He understand and completely exposes the world of self-seeking rationalists, and even coommends their philosophy to others as the prudent way of getting on in the world. His cynicism, however, does not govern his own loyalties, even though it is the means of bringing Lear to an awareness of the world to which he is now subject. Having told him that his hope of retaining kingly honour is a delusion, he proceeds to tell Lear that Goneril and Regan are identical in their attitudes towards him. Lear, however, will not be persuaded of the truth of this even when Regan greets him with the same attitude towards his age as he had found in his eldest-born:

> O, sir, you are old;
> Nature in you stands on the very verge
> Of her confine. You should be rul'd and led
> By some discretion that discerns your state.
> Better than you yourself.
>
> (II. iv. 144)

Not only is he denied the privileges of a king, but also those of a father; he must accept an inversion of the natural order. In the characteristic idiom of the Fool, Lear has made his daughters, his mothers, by giving them the rod and putting doown his own breeches.

Lear does not at once perceive the significance of this; he persists in his notions of the rights of kingship and fatherhood which had caused him to banish Cordelia and Kent. This is clear in the logic of his appeal to Regan:

> 'Tis not in thee
> To grudge my pleasures, to cut off my train,
> To bandy hasty words, to scant my sizes,
> And, in conclusion, to oppose the bolt
> Against my coming in; thou better know'st
> The offices of nature, *bond of childhood,*
> Effects of courtesy, dues of gratitude;
> *Thy half a' th' kingdom hast thou not forgot,*
> Wherein I thee endow'd.
>
> (II. iv. 172)

Retrospectively, we can see even more clearly why he misunderstood Cordelia's declaration that she loved him according to her "bond"; the irony is that she had meant it as "the bond of childhood" in the truest sense whereas Lear, then as now, confuses it with a bond as understood by a Shylock. It is now, towards the end of Act II, that Lear is forced to realize that material rewards do not secure the kind of love and respect he longs for. He claims that he had given "all" to these daughters; it is important to realize that he is referring only to the gift of his kingdom. He cannot mean that he gave all his love to his elder daughters because, as he tells Cordelia, he always loved her most. Whatever may be the misdeeds of Goneril, a "father's curse" is a contradiction in terms of natural law. One of the most painful scenes in the play is enacted as Lear tries to compromise with the same daughter whom he had left with bitter imprecations; since Goneril will allow him too retain twice as many knights as Regan will,

I'll go with thee.
Thy fifty yet doth double five and twenty,
And thou art twice her love.

(II. iv. 257)

The reiteration of his mathematical evaluation of love is at the same time "profoundly comic and profoundly pathetic."[11]

Almost at once, the comedy disappears as Lear, for the first time, speaks of himself with true humility:

You see me here, you gods, a poor old man,
As full of grief as age; wretched in both.

(II. iv. 271)

What makes this tragic rather than pathetic is that it is also a moment of great dignity for him. He saves his pride as a father by refusing to beg and cringe any longer in front of his heartless daughters. He had said to Regan, "'Tis not in thee... to oppose the bolt/Against my coming in." His error is dramatically emphasized by her being the one who gives the deeply symbolic instructioon, "Shut up your doors", which is echoed by Cornwall. From their world Lear is shut out, though he is followed by Gloucester, Kent and the Fool as he goes out into the stormy night.

The Fool is not present at Lear's love-test of his daughters, but his catchism based on the value of "nothing" is an obvious echo of it.[12] To his question, "Can you make no use of nothing, nuncle?" Lear replies without any hesitation with what, at this stage, seems to him a truism: "Why, no, boy; nothing can be made out of nothing." The masterial destitution of Lear, when he possesses "nothing", finds its first powerful visual presentation when he stands on the heath, "A poor, infirm, weak and despis'd old man." Significantly, this is also the moment when he loses his obsession with his own suffering; the object of his compassion, appropriately enough, is the Fool. "Poor fool and knave, I have one part in my heart/ That's sorry yet for thee." He had spoken with affectioon to the Fool earlier, but it had been tinged with an awareness of his being no more than the court jester, allowed to carry his critical raillery only up to a certain point; beyond that is the threat of the whip. There is no such patronizing inflection in Lear's voice now; this is the first stage in his realization of his bond with his fellow beings, his first gain from being reduced to a state of material nothingness.

So far Lear has thought of himself as a perfect king, one who discharged his royal obligations, in particular towards his daughters, by relinquishing the kingdom to them in his old age. Now, as he stands on the heath, he accepts that he has been an imperfect king, one who has taken too little care of the poor naked wretches in his kingdom. This is the first time that he convicts himself of negligence; so far he has genuinely believed that he was a man "More sinn'd against than sinning." His acknowledgement of his shortcomings as a king, and his apology to his poor subjects, is an essential preliminary to his awareness of his lack of understanding as a father, which he is later to ask Cordelia to forgive. It is now that Shakespeare by a brilliant stroke relates what might have been an impersonal and abstract reference to the miseries of "houseless poverty" to the contemporary background. Edgar as "poor Tom" is a concrete embodiment of the absolute penury of which Lear has taken too little care as King. From him Lear is to learn that though many are in his condition, the reasons for such destitution can be much more irrational than the unkindness of daughters. In spite of the interjections by Edgar, Kent, and the Fool, Lear goes on repeataing that the ingratitude of children is the essential cause of suffering. This is very similar to the pattern of his dialogue with his daughters when he conducts the love-test in Act I sc. i. Then, as now, he "determines in advance the answers he will receive; he fails to adapt himself to the person with whom he is speaking."[13] This is a particularly important point to bear in mind, because Lear is very seldom alone and ostensibly addresses his great speeches to another person actually present on the stage; this makes his isolation much more poignant.

It is as a corrective to Lear's narow grasp of human suffering and evil that Edgar's speeches here (III. iv. 50 ff.) are important. The first begins with an accusation against the injustice of society ("Who gives anything to poor Tom?"), and describes graphically the bestial life that he is compelled to lead. The second deal with the vanities and lusts of human beings, an aspect of life Lear has not known. At last Lear is forced to realize that to be deprived of a kingdom, even of the love of children, is still to be at one remvoe from the fundamental unprotectedness of man, as personified by poor Tom. "Thou art the thing itself: unaccommodated man is no more but such a poor, bare, forked animal as thou art." To prove this for himself, he strips himself to the elemental nakedness of man: "Off, off, you lendings ! Come, unbutton here." The pattern of the tragedy expands when Lear, the outcast father, and Edgar, the outcast soon, meet. This is not merely a structural synthesis of a chronicle play and a Sidneian narrative; Shakespeare gives a special relationship to these two characters: in Act II sc. i., Regan refers to Edgar as Lear's godson. On him is to rest the dual burden of bringing his godfather as well as his father to a true insight into appearance and reality. The presence of the Fool becomes superfluous now that Lear has a more sophisticated tutor to guide him in his spiritual growth.

By bringing Lear to the level of "unaccoommodated man," Edgar converts him to a state in which he becomes eager to apprehend the nature of reality. Once he has lost his reason, Lear becomes keen to talk to this philosopher, the "learned Theban." It is a childlike faith that he has in this new-found friend, and he insists on his company to continue his personal search into the meaning of existence. The basic question is asked when he tries to explain his daughters' cruelty to him: "Is there any cause in nature that make(s) these hard hearts?" His question is not within the realm of objective observation of the world, on which the cynical comments of the Fool had been based; he has moved to the realm of metapysics and in this quest Edgar, and not the Fool, is the suitable guide. In his requisition of the services of the former ("You, sir, I entertain for one of my hundred"), is implied the dismissal of the latter; that is why the Fool appears no more after this scene.

Once Lear has been made to recognize "unaccommodated man" for what he is, he coompletes the proocess of "divesting" himself initiated by him in the first scene though, of course, he had no idea then that he would be compelled to live as literal fact what he had intended only metaphcrically; the tearing off of his clothes makes him one of the "naked wretches" as impersonated by poor Tom. In the company of Edgar, Lear learns not only not to set his heart on "proud array" but comes to an awareness of its double deceptiveness. In his comment on Regan's clothes is implicit a condemnation of clothes used for ostentation or provocative vanity; they are neither the symbols of dignity nor the protective cover of chastity. The problem of appearance and reality is expressed by him in a doubly complex way;

> Through tatter'd clothes small vices do appear;
> Robes and furr'd gowns hide all.
>
> (IV. vi. 164)

Various themes of the play coalesce in this image; "tatter'd clothes" become a symbol of the kind of "plainness" of Cordelia which, in a "trice of time," had dismantled so many "folds of favour" and had made her "small fault" seem so monstrous to her father. "Robes and furr'd gowns" are a hypocritical cloak for those who will not show themselves as God made them, but only appear artificially disguised, as their tailor made them. Oswald is the typical example of this false world, and it is appropriate that he should be in the service of Goneril and Regan who first deceived Lear by clothing their treacherous thoughts in the language of fulsome flattery. Lear is not yet ready for a reconciliation with Cordelia; he must undergo a spiritual upheaval which will correct his basic perspective of values, and enable him to distinguish between truth and falsehood, between sincerity and dissimulation. His false robes must be discarded; it is in "fresh garments" that he meets Cordelia in Act IV.

An unexpected companion of Lear in his madness is Gloucester. Gloucester is not present when Lear conducts the love-test of his daughters and banishes Kent on his protesting against the verdict. At first it seems as if Gloucester has been made indignant by the report of these events.

> Kent banish'd thus ! and France in choler parted!
> And the King gone to-night! Prescrib'd his pow'r !
> Confin'd to exhibition ! All this done
> Upon the gad !
>
> (I. ii. 23)

But this turns out to be only pious rhetoric; he is no Kent to stake his fortunes on ethical principles. Soon, he has pledged his service to Regan and Cornwall, assuring them that they are "right welcome" to his caste. His mooral nataure is of the shoddiest because, although he recognizes the magnitude of the wrong done to Lear by the stocking of Kent, he makes no more than a verbal protest, offering as his excuse his subservience to Cornwall. He does not yet distinguish between loyalty and servility as Kent had done in opposing his master. Even when Lear is shut out in the stormy night, his sympathy is passive. It is an uninspring picture indeed of a man aware of the customary obligations but without the necessary courage and independence to discharge them in moments of crisis. When he finally resolves to go to the aid of the King. Shakespeare deliberately leaves his motivation ambiguous. Gloucester would like us to believe that he is prompted by pure loyalty: "If I die for it, as no less is threatened me, the King my old master must be relieved." But he has earlier revealed to us that loyalty to the King at this juncture may even be profitable; he has received secret letters, the purport of which is that "there is part of a power already footed" to revenge the injuries suffered by the King.

Buttressed thus, his resolution does not falter, and he goes in search of Lear. On the stormy heath his role as a courtier is made subsidiary to his essential nature, of which we were given a glimpse in the opening lines of the play. When Lear thought of "houseless poverty," he was immediately confronted with a concrete embodiment of his thought in poor Tom, whose first long speech catalogues the animal existence of the poor. Immediately after the Fool's simile (a little fire in a wide field is as "an old lecher's heart-- a small spark, all the rest on's body cold"), Gloucester enters, "pat! ... like the catastrophe of the old comedy." The allusion to lechery is intentional, because he, like Lear, believes himself to be a father more sinned against than sinning. In exposing the baselessness of this complacency, Edgar's assumed madness in this scene becomes very similar to Hamlet's "antic disposition."[14] In his choric speeches before the arrival of Gloucester, he admits the duty of children to their parents, but subtly implies that there are obligations on the other side also. In his mock description of himself, the essential baseness of the "serving-man," one who "serv'd the lust of my mistress' heart, and did the act of darkness with her;" is stressed. There is a *double entendre* of the most comprehensive kind here; Edgar is at the same time castigating the past of his father, and the future of his brother. Edgar has been the victim of his father's lust; like the false daughters of Lear, Edmund gets his reward in material terms for being master enough of "the glib and oily art" to take in his father. Both fathers must be made to realize that there are more sins on their heads than are dreamt of in their philosophy.

The contrast between the father who has been led by the

ingratitude of his children to reduce himself to the level of "unaccommodated man," and the father who has yet shown no such signs of havoc but, on the contrary, comes from the Court smug in the sense of his "charity," is almost comic. He greets Lear with what must be a masterpiece of aphoristic anticlimax in dramatic literature:

> Our flesh and blood, my lord, is grown so vile
> That is doth hate what gets it.
>
> (III. iv. 141)

At last he has come to do his duty by Lear, but it is too late; Lear is engaged in a search in which he needs the guidance of his "philosopher," and not of this tiresome old man harping on his charity and, even more ludicrously, comparing his so far undisturbed sanity--"because the sane buy their peace of mind by adjusting themselves to the received ideas of society"[15]--to the madness of Lear. Gloucester is no tragic hero; his suffering does not lead him to any exploration of the fundamental questions of life. Once he is told of his mistaken trust in Edmund he accepts this with as little question as he had earlier accepted the report of Edgar's treachery. This is characteristic oof him throughout; his nature is much more limited than that of Lear, so he can quite simply say:

> Then Edgar was abus'd
> Kind gods, forgive me that, and prosper him.
>
> (III. vii. 90)

Instead of achieving spiritual growth through suffering, he evades the issue by taking refuge in a facile pessimism:

> As files to wanton boys are we to th' gods--
> They kill us for their sport.
>
> (IV. i. 37)

His renunciation of the world, culminating in his resolve to commit suicide is, unlike Lear's, born of a desire to escape suffering. It is from this that Edgar rescues him to an adult philosophy of endurance, a variation in a minor key on the theme of Lear's spiritual regeneration.

> Henceforth I'll bear
> Affliction till it do cry out itself
> 'Enough, enough' and die.
>
> (IV. vi. 75)

Edgar has indeed been his guide, who has led him, begged for him, and saved him from despair. Until the end, Gloucester incapable of grappling with the extremes of human experience that Lear has to grapple with to his dying breath; characteristically, his heart proves too weak to sustain the conflict between "two extremes of passion, joy and grief," and it bursts "smilingly."

For Lear there is no facile reconciliation with Cordelia. To repent for his misunderstanding of her is one thing, to confront her and ask for her forgiveness is another. Kent reports his predicament:

> A sovereign shame so elbows him; his own unkindness,
> That stripp'd her from his benediction, turn'd her
> To foreign casualties, gave her dear rights
> To his dog-hearted daughters--these things sting
> His mind so venomously that burning shame
> Detains him from Cordelia.
>
> (IV. iii. 42)

This is the culmination of the agonized process of self-knowledge that he had embarked on. After a restorative sleep, in his "fresh garaments," he is ready to receive the love of Cordelia. We realize now the reason for his shame; he was ready to ask for her forgiveness, but his view of the bond between them is still so much in terms of cause and effect that he feared she would bear a grudge against him, the justice of which he would not be able to refuse. He has to learn from her that the bond of love is not a conditional one. Whatever he may have done to her, she sees no breach between them; she is still his child, her "I am, I am being characteristic in its simplicity. She admits no cause that would justify the wronging of a father by his child. In his kneeling to her is the acknowledgement of a different kind of hierarchical propriety from the one which made him think that a father had the right to "price" his daughter in terms of a share of a kingdom. He had gone beyond the prerogative of a father in declaring:

> Here I disclaim all my paternal care
> Propinquity and property of blood,
> And as a stranger to my heart and me
> Hold thee from this for ever.
>
> (I. i. 112)

Cordelia has been true to her "bond"; when she had left her father to the care of her sisters, she had be sought them to love him; there was no recrimination then, and there is none now. The visual impact of Lear kneeling to beg her forgiveness is as powerful as that of Volumnia kneeling to her son in *Coriolanus;* the action marks a reversal in which love is recognized as the supreme value, before which no sacrifice in terms of pride is excessive. In Lear's case this is particularly significant as it recalls a similar posture of mock humility in front of Regan, at a time when the acceptance of such a reversal of hierarchical propriety was inconceivable to him. His desire for vengeance, expressed in the terrible cry, "kill, kill, kill, kill, kill, kill!" is now forgotten. He has no desire to even see "these daughters and these sisters." In his vision of his life with Cordelia, prison becomes a heaven of love:

> We two alone will sing like birds i' th' cage;
> When thou dost ask me blessing, I'll knee down
> And ask of thee forgiveness;
>
> (V. iii. 9)

This is a "willed isolation" indeed but it is not due to a failure on his part to come to a realization of the "waste he has wrought."[16] Rather it is born of an almost mystical apprehension of a personal search for the meaning of love and forgiveness which is by its very nature to be pursued in isolation.

But is this renuion only a grim joke played by the gods on Lear? The scene must be related to its emotional context to be properly understood; there is deep tragic irony here. Lear wants to believe that, by renouncing the world, he and Cordelia will put themselves beyond the power of evil; this is the illusion that is broken by Edmund's order that Cordelia be hanged. In spite of the sacrifices they have made, Lear and his youngest daughter are not to find their heaven of love in this world. Lear knows that Cordelia has no life at all, yet he refuses to accept their separation as final. He is sure she must have a message for him; once before, he had lost her because of his failure to understand what she had said in her gentle and low voice, and he is determined not to repeat his error. He is convinced that she is trying to say something to him and, at last, he understands what the movement of her lips means; when this world has struck its final blow, there is hope of another world of "the mystery of things."[17] That is where he will join her; if they would "undo this button" his breath would escape the sooner. It is as an epilogue to this that Kent's final gesture of loyalty is meaningful:

> I have a journey, sir, shortly to go
> My master calls me; I must not say no.
>
> (V. iii. 321)

It is only this kind of "bond" that survives to the end for Lear, who was the focal point of multiple relationships at the beginning of the play. The setting of the final scene is deliberately the same as that of the first; this serves to emphasize the tragic evolution of Lear from a man obsessed with the symbols of his social position to a titanic figure of suffering and renunciation.

REFERENCES

1. *Shakespearean Tragedy,* p. 263.
2. *Johnson on Shakespeare,* ed. W. Raleigh (Oxford, 1908), p. 162. Johnson is here supporting the view of Mr. Murphy, "a very judicious critic."
3. W.M.T. Nowottny, "Lear's Questions," *Shakespeare Survey,* 10 (1957), p. 91.

4. G. Bush, *Shakespeare and the Natural Condition* (Harvard, 1956), p. 94.

5. R.B. Heilman, *This Great Stage* (Baton Rouge, 1948), p. 36.

6. See E.A. Block, "*King Lear*: A Study of Balanced and Shifting Sympathies," *Shakespeare Quarterly, X* (1959), esp. p. 504.

7. H. Granville-Barker, *Prefaces to Shakespeare* (London, 1963), Vol. II, p. 50.

8. J. Stampfer, "The Catharsis of *King Lear,*" *Shakespeare Survey,* 13 (1960), p. 6.

9. J.A. Barish and M. Waingrow, " 'Service' in *King Lear,*" *Shakespeare Quarterly,* IX (1958), p. 349, authors' italics.

10. *Op. cit.* esp. pp. 135-143.

11. G. Wilson Knight, *The Wheel of Fire,* p. 161.

12. I agree with William Empson, *Seven Types of Ambiguity* (3rd edition, London, 1956, p. 45, that this is an example of Shakespeare's ironies meant for "the pleasure rather of commentators than of first-night audiences." However, it seems to me that in *The Structure of Complex Words* (London, 1952), pp. 138-139, he is unnecessarily diffident about relating this to the theme of renunciation in the play. See George Orwell, "Lear, Tolstoy, and the Fool," in *Collected Essays* (London, 1961).

13. W.H. Clemen, *The Development of Shakespeare's Imagery,* p. 134.

14. See J.F. Danby, *Shakespeare's Doctrine of Nature* (London, 1949), p. 151.

15. K. Muir, "Madness in *King Lear,*" *Shakespeare Survey* 13 (1960), p. 38.

16. J. Lawlor, *The Tragic Sense in Shakespeare,* p. 171.

17. Philip Edwards, *Shakespeare and the Confines of Art* (London, 1968), p. 132, denies this: "If Shakespeare had wished to say this, he could have said it." I think enough *is* said, especially by Kent.

5

Antony and Cleopatra

The main protagonists in *Antony and Cleopatra* are conceived on a scale that sets them apart from the other characters in the play. Hyperbole is the natural mode of expression of the main protagonists, for each other and for their love. He is the "demi-Atlas of the earth," a "rare spirit"; she is a "lass unparallel'd" whom "age cannot wither." To set a limit to their love, there must be found a "new heaven, new earth"; it is measured in terms of kingdoms, which are no more than "clay" when compared to its "nobleness." Our imagination responds to the grand gestures that come easily to the lovers--Antony rating a tear of Cleopatra's above all that is won and lost; she sucking an asp to be true to herself and Antony, and contemptuously renouncing this world which is "not worth leave-taking."

These are the memorable impressions, but obviously they do not sum up the play. The love of Antony and Cleopatra is not like that of Romeo and Juliet, on which the shadws cast are of external forces; the trust between the young and innocent lovers remains untranished, and they do not regret the social ostracism that they suffer. After all, what's in aname? The names of Montague and Capulet are merely the symbols of artificially exaggerated differences between two noble families of Verona, hence it is easy to "doff" them for an ecstatic love. In the love of Antony and Cleopatra, the stake is tremendous: the sacrifice not only of a name but also of an empire. The love story is raised to epic level by the lovers being symbolic of two contending worlds: Antony is the "Herculean Roman," Cleopatra is often called "Egypt." The play is made complex, if not bewildering, by Shakespeare's attempt to portray a personal relationship between the main characters set against, and inextricably linked with, political events. And the political world here is totally decadent; as we watch the ignoble struggle for power in Rome, "a painful sense of hollowness oppresses us."[1] The question that arisesthen in respect of Antony's love is: is it of a piece with this "hollowness," or is it worthy of the sacrifice of his position in imperial Rome that he offers to it?

Antony himself does not seem to be sure of the answer: he vacillates between two contradictory attitudes towards his love. His moments of happiness are identified with a complete faith in the glory of his love, its harmony with his honour, so that he can confidently condemn the kingdoms he has given up for it as mere clay. From this he veers, on suspecting Cleopatra of faithlessness or himself of dishonourable conduct, to complete despair in feeling himself bereft of affection or power. This movement characterizes the play, the pendulum of emotion finally coming to rest in the unclouded vision of an immortality of love with which the lovers die. This movement is not, however, characterized by "repetition and monotony."[2] Antony's despair is each time more bitter, because each time he has disownedyet another tie or claim for Cleopatra's sake, and his dependence on her love is proportionately greater. It would be a mistake to think of him as a romantic lover who spontaneously and unquestioningly rejects all else for his love. His isolation from his social and political milieu is gradual, and falls into three distinct stages. In the first, up to Act III sc. iv, he attempts to retain his political position in Rome. The second is initiated in Act III sc. vi, when his return to Cleopatra is announced. From Act III sc. vii to sc xii, he tries to win power by fighting against Caesar with the help of some loyal Roman followers and Cleopatra's army. Only after the battle of Actium does he accept that his sword must obey his affection "on all cause." This final surrender to his love for Cleopatra, and the rejection of all other ambitions, is expressed in his farewell to his soldiers and in his request to Caesar to be allowed to live as "a private man in Athens."

The reasons for this pattern of development lie as much in Antony's character as in external forces. He is no congenital scorner of the common people as Coriolanus is; he is a gregarious temperament, which finds its most satisfying expression in conviviality. He is no devotee of abstract principles, though he is capable of the ultimate sacrifice for the love of a woman. That is why his isolation is not as absolute as that of Macbeth or Coriolanus. He breaks some ties, but only to form one that gives full scope to his natural love of pleasure, feasting and splendour. Had Cleopatra betrayed him at the end, his isolation would have been 'tragic' in the limited sense. But she is ultimately faithful to him; out of his isolation is born a greater bond than either of them has known before. We hardly ever see Antony alone; what would have been expressed in soliloquy by a hero like Hamlet is expressed by him in the presence of Cleopatra or Enobarbus. Only at the moment when he is contemplating suicide does he feel himself completely forsaken, but he dies with his love for Cleopatra paramount in his mind, all other ties forgotten. He, like Coriolanus, dies away from Rome, but he is not torn to pieces by treacherous enemies: he dies "a Roman by a Roman valiantly vanquish'd"; the land in which he is enemy country to Rome, as is Corioli, but for him it is a symbol of his love, his "Egypt."

The first half of the play is concerned with Antony's attempts to reinstate himself as a leader in Rome. That this will involve the giving up of his love for Cleopatra is clear to us from the opening speech of the play; the Roman-Egyptian antithesis[3] is implicit in it. Philo laments that the heart of Antony, the great Roman captain,

> Which in the scuffles of great fights hath burst
> The buckles on his breast, reneges all temper,
> And is become the bellows and the fan
> To cool a gipsy's lust.
>
> (I. i. 7)

Certainly, the Romans do not see any "nobleness" in this love of Antony's; in their eyes it is nothing but animal lust. Caesar would not object to his desire to "tumble on the bed of Ptolemy," if Rome did not have to bear "so great weight in his lightness." But as he is "the triple pillar of the world," Caesar feels justified in imposing his own conditions for the continuation of their political alliance. Antony realizes the instability of his political status after the death of Fulvia; in Act I sc. ii he discusses with Enobarbus the political pressures that necessitate his return to Rome, particularly the danger that Sextus Pompeius may be invested with the dignities of his father. To Cleopatra he offers the same explanation of his departure, though he gives her assurances not implied in his conversation with Enobarbus:

> By the fire
> That quickens Nilus' slime, I go from hence
> Thy soldier, servant, making peace or war
> As thou affects.
>
> (I. iii. 68)

Once he is in Rome, his tone to Caesar is apologetic, even about the contemptuous dismissal of Caesar's messengers that we have seen in the opening scene; Antony's anxiety to heal the breach is obvious in the diplomatic, and not quite truthful, apology that he offers for the incident. An even more surprising political compromise is his marriage to Octavia. There are no illusions about the motives behind this; Caesar uses his sister as a pawn in the political game: she is to "join our kingdoms and our hearts." Obviously, Antony has had accond thoughts about scoring kingdoms as clay, and is prepared to match the diplomacy and hypocrisy of the other members of the triumvirate. Antony is certainly a martial hero at the beginning of the play but the rejection of ignoble political compromise that characterizes the heroes of Shakespeare's major tragedies does not as yet come naturally to him.

In Act II sc. vi and sc. vii, we see Antony at one with the leaders of Rome, and this unity seems purchased at a heavy cost. Unlike Coriolanus, he does not respect the sanctity of the laws of hospitality; he engages in political intrigue against Pompey even while he acknowledges that Pompey had courteously welcomed his mother to Sicily. He indulges in crude humour at the expense of Lepidus, and in drunken revelry at what aspires to be an Alexandrian feast; Shakespeare has given us here an unsparing picture of what the glory of Rome has degenerated to. Antony "in great men's fellowship" is certainly not an attractive character; the words of the Soothsayer ring true:

> The daemon, that thy spirit which keeps thee, is
> Noble, courageous, high, unmatchable,
> Where Caesar's is not; but near him thy angel
> Becomes a fear, as being o'erpow'r'd.
>
> (II. iii. 20)

Antony finds in the words of the Soothsayer a confirmation of what he has been feeling; the impossibility of enduring either a political association with Caesar, or a political marriage with Octavia. He decides to return to Egypt, and to break these Roman ties; from now on we see Antony, the Roman' in Egypt. As Coriolanus cannot come to terms with his contemporary Romans, and regally declares, "I banish you," so Antony becomes an exile when he cannot abide by a political compromise that demands the sacrifice of his love for Cleopatra, or of his honour as a soldier.

However, in exile, Antony is not as isolated from Romans as Coriolanus is; in his camp at Actium he has some loyal Roman soldiers with him. Plutarch gives a very special reason for their loyalty: Antony "being given to love, that made him the more desired; and by that means he brought many to love him. For he would further every man's love, and also would not be angry that men should merrily tell him of those he loved."[4] Shakespeare follows Plutarch in establishing a connection between Antony's propensity to love and the hero-worship this elicits from his soldiers. They do not supply to Antony the moral standards of the Roman nobility; on the contrary, they bask in the reflected splendour of their general's love. The attitude of Enobarbus in his comment on Antony's wish that he had never seen Cleopatra is typical in this respect: "O sir, you had then left unseen a wonderful piece of work, which not to have been blest withal would have discredited your travel." The various descriptions of Cleopatra and her world by Enobarbus are not merely choric; they are in character, and express the effect of the dazzling splendour of Egypt and its Queen, the extravagance of oriental feasting and lightness of heart, on the Roman soldiers who accompanied Antony. One of the most striking contrasts in the play is that between soldiers like Maecenas, who have stayed in Rome and are therefore unsympathetic to Antony's passion for Cleopatra, and those like Enobarbus who have also fallen under the spell of "Egypt." Having seen Cleopatra, Enobarbus knows that, to Antony, Octavia will seem "of a holy, cold, and still conversation." To men like him, Antony is no less a man for "condemning Rome" and returning to Egypt; they are quite happy to remain loyal to him and to aid him in his wars against Caesar.

In fighting these wars, the soldiers want Antony to continue to be their undisputed leader; they do not approve of his deference to Cleopatra in matters of war. Though they approve of the relationship, they are Roman enough to think of it in terms of animal lust, best kept away from martial enterprises. It is in such terms that Enobarbus would reply to Cleopatra's query why she should not go to the wars with Antony:

> If we should serve with horse and mares together
> The horse were merely lost; the mares would bear
> A soldier and his horse.
>
> (III. vii. 7)

The disagreement becomes even more serious when a matter of strategy is involved; all the men try to dissuade Antony from fighting by sea, but he is influenced by Cleopatra's optimism that her sixty sails are a match for Caesar's. A man like Canidius feels his loyalty weaken when he realizes that "our leader's led/And we are women's men." The flight of Cleopatra from the fight, and Antony's in pursuit of her, proves the last straw; it seems to the soldiers that they never saw

> an action of such shame;
> Experience, manhood, honour, ne'er before
> Did violate so itself.
>
> (III. x. 22)

Canidius feels that Antony has forfeited all claims to their loyalty, and decides to desert him and go over to Caesar's camp; although Enobarbus makes an effort to remain loyal, his reason tells him to follow Canidius' example.

Antony himself is acutely aware that by his dishonour on the battlefield he has "instructed cowards/To run and show their shoulders." He acknowledges that he can no longer sustain a public role as a martial leader; the "supremacy" of his love for Cleopatra has created a crisis which he must resolve at the personal level. He alone must face his problem; he has no right to involve his soldiers. That is why he sorrowfully bids them:

> Friends, be gone;

> I have myself resolv'd upon a course
> Which has no need of you; be gone.
>
> (III. xi. 8)

With this realization, Antony gives up the attempt to retain any kind of political power, and his request to Caesar is to be allowed to live as a "private man" in Athens. In his resolution to bear his personal sufferings with courage, he acquires a greater dignity, as indicated by the nature of his challenge to Caesar:

> I dare him therefore
>
> To lay his gay comparisons apart,
>
> And answer me declin'd, sword against sword,
>
> Ourselves alone.
>
> (III. xiii. 25)

Antony's isolation from Rome is not limited to the human level, the god from whom his family claimed to be descended deserts him too. The use of supernatural portents as a commentary on the dramatic action is common to all three of Shakespeare's Roman plays. There is the elements upheaval on the night of Julius Caesar's murder, and the laughter of the gods which makes Coriolanus accept the supremacy of natural ties over pride. In *Antony and Cleopatra* the supernatural is used specifically to emphasize the isolation of the hero. Shakespeare found in Plutarch the idea of Antony being forsaken by divine powers; after he had bade farewell to his soldiers,

> when all the city was quite, full of fear and sorrow, thinking what would be the issue and end of this war, it is said that suddenly they heard a marvellous sweet harmony of sundry sorts of instruments of music, with the cry of a multitude of people, as they had been dancing and had sung as they use in Bacchus' feasts, with movings and turnings after the manner of the Satyrs. And it seemed that this dance went through the city unto the gate that opened to the enemies, and that

> all the troop that made this noise they heard went out of the city at that gate. Now such as in reason sought the depth of the interpretation of this wonder thought that it was the god unto whom Antonius bare singular devotion to counterfeit and resemble him, that did forsake them.[5]

Shakespeare combines this with a much earlier passage in which Antony's patron god is clearly identified as Hercules:

> Now it had been a speech of old time that the family of the Antonii were descended from one Anton, the son of Hercules, whereof the family took name. This opinion did Antonius seek to confirm in all his doings, not only resembling him in the likeness of his body, as we have said before, but also in the wearing of his garments.[6]

The two passages are condensed to the ethereal, *Tempest*-like poetry of the scene (IV. iii) which conveys the absolute break of the "Herculean Roman" with the gods of his country: "the god Hercules, whom Antony lov'd/Now leaves him." It is entirely appropriate that the omen should be heard and interpreted by the soldiers, since Antony's farewell to them is his acknowledgement of the supremacy of his affection over his sword. The connection is explicit when he reproaches Cleopatra:

> Egypt, thou knew'st too well
> My heart was to thy rudder tied by th' strings,
> And thou shouldst tow me after. O'er my spirit
> Thy full supremacy thou knew'st, and that
> Thy beck might from the bidding of the gods
> Command me.
>
> (III. xi. 56)

Here, the bidding of the gods whom he had been brought up to worship was to stay and fight; in following Cleopatra from the battlefield he had disregarded it. Antony feels his desolation acutely in this respect when Caesar too seems to scorn him:

> He makes me angry;

> And at this time most easy 'tis to do't,
> When my good stars, that were my former guides,
> Have empty left their orbs and shot their fires
> Into th' abysm of hell.
>
> (III. xiii. 143)

Dramatically, this shifts the interest from Antony the political leader and warrior to Antony in his personal relationships as lover and friend.

There is implicit in the play a subtle Roman syllogism based on the premise that masculinity expresses itself in warrior honour as well as in complete rationality of conduct. By surrendering to his "affection," Antony is compelled to subordinate not only his "sword" but, according to this logic, also his "reason."[7] The spokesman for this Roman attitude is Enobarbus, in his reply to Cleopatra's question whether she or Antony was to blame for the fight from the sea-fight:

> Antony only, that would make his will
> Lord of his reason. What though you fled
> From that great face of war, whose several ranges
> Frighted each other? Why should he follow?
> *The itch of his affection should not then*
> *Have nick'd his captainship*, at such a point,
> When half to half the world oppos'd be being
> The mered question.
>
> (III. xiii. 3)

Enobarbus is indulgent towards his leader's "dotage" but he regards Cleopatra as a rather delectable "Egyptian dish" and no more. His metaphors for their relationship are always arrestingly vivid, but hardly refined or elevated; he speaks with the "Roman tongue,"[8] however picturesque it may be. The choric commentary of Enobarbus has a dual dramatic function; in Rome he tries to convey to the Romans the glamour of Egypt, but in Egypt he is a representative of the Roman ethic, which condemns subservience of reason to emotion as unmanly. It is on the relative importance of emotion and reason that Enobarbus and Antony disagree, and ultimately part. The emphasis on the fate of a minor character is often in Shakespeare's tragedies, the means of supplementing and illuminating our reaction to the major characters; Enobarbus is used by Shakespeare to act as a foil to Antony in his reaction to the conflict between reason and emotion. At first he resists the dictates of reason and does not desert Antony when Canidius does. But when Antony makes the heroic gesture of challenging Caesar to single combat, Enobarbus feels that his master's "judgment" has been completely subdued. This is too much for the rationalist in him and he too decides to desert Antony and go over to Caesar's camp. Another "whom Antony lov'd/Now leaves him."

With disbelief, Antony hears that his best friend has joined Caesar; to us it comes as no surprise since we have listened to Enobarbus' rationalization of his disloyalty, in spite of his awareness that to follow Antony in his misfortune would earn him "a place i' th' story." Antony knows no such calculated moves; the grand gesture comes to him easily, and he "continues still a Jove." The Romans and their gods have deserted him, but this has not diminished his god-like bounty: he orders that Enobarbus' treasures be sent after him. The magnanimity of the leader and friend to whom he had turned traitor, makes his guilt unbearable to Enobarbus. In life he has been false to his leader; in death he will redeem himself by acknowledging that, having betrayed Antony in his moment of defeat, he has deserved the stigma of being ranked forever as "a master-leaver and a fugitive." He realizes the full depth of his loyalty to his master only after leaving him, so that out of the traitorous act is born a deeper emotion, and Enobarbus finally rejects the baseness generated by following the command of reason, and dies in a noble manner, true to Antony in spirit.

The on rush of emotion in the heart of this Roman who prides himself on his bluff lack of sentiment is no sudden metamorphosis. The scene has been enacted before in a minor key, but significantly placed and presented. In Act IV sc. ii, Shakespeare follows Plutarch in his account of Antony's emotional farewell to his servants after the rejection of his challenge by Caesar:

> So, being at supper as it is reported, he commanded his officers and household servants, that waited on him at his board, that they should fill his cups full, and make as much of him as they could.
> 'For,' said he, 'you know not whether you shall do so much for me tomorrow or not, or whether you shall serve another master; and it may be you shall see me no more, but a dead body.' This notwithstanding, perceiving that his friends and men fell a-weeping to hear him say so, to salve that he had spoken he added this more unto it: that he would not lead them to battle where he thought not rather safely toreturn with victory than valiantly to die with honour.[9]

Here, no mention is made of any servant by name, and the traitorous original of Shakespeare's Enobarbus[10] is dead long before this. Shakespeare has Enobarbus present here, and makes this last scene of his with his master brilliantly ironical Antony has no inkling of the betrayal we have seen his debating, so he treats Enobarbus with the same *camaraderie* as always. In his last battle he assumes that Enobarbus will fight well, since he is assured by him: "I'll strike, and cry 'Take all'." In the actual farewell, the emphasis is on Enobarbus' reaction to Antony's generous acknowledgement of the service and loyalty of his followers. To none would this be more applicable than to Enobarbus, but Antony does not know the need to bid him farewell, though we do. Enobarbus is still blind enough to dismiss the expression of his loyalty as effeminate:

> What mean you, sir,
> To give them this discomfort? Look, they weep;
> And I, an ass, am onion-ey'd. For shame!
> Transform us not to women.
>
> (IV. ii. 33)

His idiom when speaking about emotion has not changed from the time when he had advised that the tears from an onion should water Antony's sorrow at Fulvia's death. Antony has changed since then, and has acknowledged the supremacy of affection over manly reason; by being with him, Enobarbus has changed too, but he does not know it. His minor tragedy is played out as he first contemptuously scorns his love for Antony, in the same way that he has throughout cynically exposed the emotions of others; too late does he find out that faith is not mere folly. The hero suffers the pain of isolation but those who desert him do not automatically find happiness; betrayal exacts its own penalties.

With the desertion of Enobarbus, Antony loses his last personal link with the Roman world. The stage is now clear for the development of the Antony-Cleopatra relationship, without any important political or emotional digression. By a brilliant stroke of dramatic irony, Shakespeare has her present at the scene of Antony's farewell to his servants. She and Enobarbus are separated from the rest of the group and carry on a conversation in asides; both of them have intentions of betraying Antony, yet they are moved. Here, in their whispering asides, these two, in whom Antony has reposed love and trust, assume a conspiratorial air. Enobarbus betrays him and joins Caesar; the question now is--will Cleopatra, who has been wooed so eagerly by Caesar, follow his example? Will she accept the compromise that Rome offers her, or will she justify Antony's isolation from Rome by following with allegiance her fallen lord?

Shakespeare takes from Plutarch the main outlines of Cleopatra character, but there is a subtle though significant difference between the emphasis of the dramatist and the historian. Plutarch goes out of his way to be fair to her, but as soon as she is mentioned be makes his overall moral judgment about her quite explicit:

> Antonius being thus inclined, the last and extremist mischief of all other (to wit, the love of Cleopatra) lighted on him, who did waken and stir up many vices yet hidden in him, and were never seen to any; and, if any spark of goodness or hope of rising were left him, Cleopatra quenched it straight and made it worse than before.[11]

Having stated this, Plutarch proceeds to describe the enchantment of Antony by her. Shakespeare subtly alters this mode of presentation: the disapproving Plutarchan point of view, expressed by Philo, is eclipsed by the richly imaginative poetry that is given to the lovers at their first entrance. To Cleopatra's provocative, "I'll set a bourn how far to be belov'd", Antony replies: "Then must thou needs find out new heaven, new earth." Antony speaks here with an assurance that, we find out later, is not constant. In their love, he asserts, they stand up peerless. She tries to taunt him with his Roman obligations, but he refuses to attend to such prosaic matters. We feel her "infinite variety" through the intoxication of Antony:

> Fie, wrangling queen!
> Whom everything becomes--to chide, to laugh,
> To weep; whose every passion fully strives
> To make itself in thee fair and admir'd.
>
> (I. i. 48)

Only after having established her thus in our imagination does Shakespeare give dramatic emphasis to the other side of the picture.

This is represented by Cleopatra's court, the decadent frivolity of which is effectively dramatized in the next scene. The dialogue is steeped in sexual innuendo; appropriately, the presiding deity is Isis, the Egyptian name for Venus.[12] The identification of Cleopatra with the goddess is a simple dramatic inference; she is the queen of love trying to ensnare Antony's heart, as she had ensnared those of his Roman predecessors. She speaks of these triumps often in the play, even at moments when she is ostensibly longing for Antony in his absence. When she first appears with Antony, there is the lyricism of love in her language, but this is no more than the perfection of the courtesan's art. She can match Antony's hyperbole, but she is not in love yet. She enjoys her voluptuous languishing for Antony while he is away in Rome; it brings back flattering memories of another great Roman she had "loved." In the beginning, when Antony is still Roman enough to want to break "these Egyptian fetters" he does not seem to mind the fact that he is only one of a series of Cleopatra's Roman lovers; since he himself regards the relationship as temporary, this is only natural.

It is when Antony leaves Cleopatra, and marries Octavia, that the strength of his attachment to her becomes apparent to him. Of course, there are political motives for his return to Egypt, but these are not made paramount in the play. The substance of the Soothsayer's advice is borrowed from Plutarch, but Antony's reaction to it is very different. In the *Life* he makes the politically adequate gesture of leaving Italy and going to Greece with Octavia, in order to make space enough between himself and Caesar; he lives there for three years, and has children by Octavia. In the play, he immediately decides to return to the East, Cleopatra his chief motive. He knows what social privileges he has forfeited for her sake; as he reminds her when she threatens to be unfaithful,

> Have I my pillow left unpress'd in Rome,
> Forborne the getting of a lawful race,
> And by a gem of women, to be abus'd
> By one that looks on feeders?
>
> (III. xiii. 106)

Once he gives up his empire, or whatever share of it he could have salvaged by compromising with Caesar, he expects Cleopatra to reciprocate by giving up the kind of amorous-cum-political intrigues she had engaged in with his predecessors.

When Antony has accepted the status of a "private man," he takes it for granted that Cleopatra will be loyal to him. Thus, when his messenger returns from Rome, he refers Caesar's reply to her, sure that she will not even consider the terms that have been offered:

> The Queen shall then have courtesy, so she
> Will yield us up...
> Let her know't.
>
> (III. xiii. 15)

Betrayal by her now, when he has disowned all else for her, is inconceivable to him; that is why he is shocked when he comes upon her currying favour with Caesar's ambassador. As he feels this last support withdrawn, a sense of desolation overwhelms him.

> Now, gods and devils!
> Authority melts from me. Of late, when I cried 'Ho!'
> Like boys unto a muss, kings would start forth
> And cry 'Your will?' Have you no ears? I am
> Antony yet.
>
> (III. xiii. 89)

Antony, The most extrovert of Shakespeare's major tragic heroes begins to develop a sense of identity which is not dependent upon the numerous relationship through which he has projected himself so far. His sense of betrayal by Cleopatra compels him to attempt a recognition of his essential self. Feeling that all is lost, he tries to comprehend the magnitude of human disloyalty:

> All come to this? The hearts
> That spaniel'd me at heels, to whom I gave
> Their wishes, do discandy, melt their sweets
> On blossoming Caesar; and this pine is bark'd
> That overtopp'd them all.
>
> (IV. xii. 20)

From the general indictment, Antony proceeds to the particular; betrayal by others he has accepted, and even forgiven, but betrayal by Cleopatra, for whom he had given up all, threatens him with total disintegration of personality:

> O this false soul of Egypt! this grave charm--
> Whose eye beck'd forth my wars and call'd them home,
> Whose bosom was my crowne, my chief end--
> Like a right gipsy hath at fast and loose
> Beguil'd me to the very heart of loss.
>
> (IV. xii. 24)

She had beguiled him of his empire and his reputation, but that he had forgiven her when assured of her love; her treachery in 'selling' him to Caesar he cannot. In keeping with her characterization her guilt here is left ambiguous but, remembering her manner towards Thyreus, Caesar's ambassador, we can well believe her capable of this 'policy.' Antony reacts here like Othello when he wrongly believes himself beguiled by Desdemona; the characters of the two heroes are very different, as are those of the women by whom they believe themselves to be betrayed, but the elemental anguish is recognizably similar. To Othello the unbearable thought is:

> But there, where I have garner'd up my heart,
> Where either I must live or bear no life,
> The fountain from the which my current runs,
> Or else dries up--to be discarded thence!
>
> (*Othello*, IV. ii. 58)

If in such love there can be falsehood, the whole universe is rendered meaningless. Antony's entire being had come to be centered in Cleopatra; with this support withdrawn he is bewildered by his loss of identity: "Here I am Antony;/Yet cannot hold this visible shape." There is no point or purpose in life any more; the only consolation is in the forlorn resolve:

> ...there is left us
> Ourselves to end ourselves.
>
> (IV. xiv. 21)

But Antony is saved from such a lonely death. The

pendulum of emotion swings yet again, the movement this time initiated by Cleopatra with her false message of her death. Since the final consummation is to come after Antony's death, his reaction to this pretence, which he does not know to be so, gives us, through a brilliant stroke of dramatic skill, his response to Cleopatra's sacrifice to love which matches his. When he believes that Cleopatra has died, with his name on her lips at the end, he forgets all his suspicions of her treachery; his only desire is to join her in the world "where souls do couch on flowers." The deception, when he discovers it, does not arouse any bitterness in him, and should arouse none in us, as Antony is not here deluded but is merely trusting her protestations of love and grief, which confidence she justifies after his death. Antony has not a word of regret for the domestic, political and martial ties he had broken for Cleopatra's sake; at the end he feels that his isolation is redeemed, as he envisions an immortality of love with her.

This mood is not disturbed when Antony learns that her message was false; all he wants now is to be carried "where Cleopatra bides." As before, a kiss will repay him for all that he has lost, but it is not equally certain that a kiss from him is as precious to her. She is unwilling to descend from the monument and risk her safety; she has still not accepted that love makes demands which involve sacrifices. Since the beginning of their relationship, she has imposed her conditions upon Antony; even now she does not change the pattern, as she insists that he be drawn up into the monument. Compared to the simplicity of his "I am dying, Egypt, dying," her grief sounds theatrical; we are not sure that this is not a more sublime example of her histrionic ability. But when she states that her honour and her safety "do not go together" we seem to detect a new note in her voice. Is the poignancy of the moment--the realization of the great love for which this Roman had given up an empire--creating a more heroic concept of honour in her? There is only a hint, but it is significantly placed, just before Antony's epitaph spoken by himself. Like the other Roman hero, Coriolanus, death comes to him away from his countrymen, and he must assert for the reassurance of himself and his love, the glory of his career as it had been. He is proud that he has not cowardly put off his "helmet" to his "countrymen"; had he done that, and returned to Rome, we have in his words to Eros (IV. xiv. 73 ff.) a graphic account of how he would have been treated. His spirit, even when it is going, has not shrunk to the size of any of those that have betrayed him. Does he include Cleopatra among them? We are not told definitely.

In the *Life,* Proculeius enters at "the last gasp" of Antonius,[13] and the interest shifts to Caesar's lament for Antony and his designs upon Cleopatra. But Shakespeare focuses our attention on Cleopatra's reaction to Antony's death; before our eyes her personality acquires a new dimension as she is overcome by the desolation of her loss;

> Noblest of men, woo't die?
> Hast thou no care of me? Shall I abide
> In this dull world, which in thy absence is
> No better than a sty?
>
> (IV. xv. 59)

This is not the idiom of the courtesan we have seen so far, albeit a regal one; her regality, in her grief, is of no value. As Antony had become bereft of all except his personal dignity, so she feels now no more "but e'en a woman." She rises in stature as she scorns political compromise with Caesar and determines to join Antony in death. The resolution made now wavers in the implementation of it, but we must not doubt the genuiness of it here:

> ...what's brave, what's noble,
> Let's do it after the high Roman fashion,
> And make death proud to take us.
>
> (IV. xv. 86)

She, who had resented the moments when "a Roman thought" had struck Antony, for the first time identifies herself with the "Roman fashion." Only now, in her acceptance of some of Antony's values, is she unequivocally true to him.

Will she remain true to this Roman ideal, we wonder, especially when Caesar tries to woo her with the express intention of preventing her suicide? He instructs his ambassador, Proculeius:

> Give her what comforts
> The quality of her passion shall require,
> Lest, in her greatness, by some mortal stroke
> She do defeat us; for her life in Rome
> Would be eternal in our triumph.
>
> (V. i. 62)

Act V sc. ii seems in direct sequence to Act. sc. xv in respect of the sort of mood is Cleopatra in to receive this message; she is still resolved to commit suicide:

> My desolation does begin to make
> A better life. 'Tis paltry to be Caesar:
>
> (V. ii. I)

The speech beginning with these lines is significantly placed here for emphasis; it is essential to our understandng of this much-discussed scene. Shakespeare is carefully reminding us of the new-born tragic quality of Cleopatra's character so that we should not misunderstand her obsequious manner towards Proculeius, and the Seleucus episode. She tries to deal with these political emissaries, but her perfect technique in negotiations of this kind seems irrelevant; their world seems unreal to her from the dream-like world that she has entered after the death of Antony. By surrendering to her love for him, she has indeed found a "new heaven, new earth." Her identification with Antony is now complete as she echoes the limpid quality of his hyperbolical utterance:

> His face was as the heav'ns, and therein stuck
> A sun and moon, which kept their course and lighted
> The little O, the earth.
>
> (V. ii. 79)

Her desire is to prove her love "by taking Antony's course," the very ting that Caesar is taking great pains to prevent. She has always been "cunning past man's thought," so what match is this boy Caesar for her? She will play the game, make him believe that she wants to compromise with him. She is Cleopatra enough to enjoy the joke, saying that she had been saving her treasure so that she could induce the mediation of Livia and Octavia on her behalf ! So she "finely deceiveth Octavius Caesar, as though she desired to live."

To live to endure political disgrace is impossible for her; her growth as a woman is indicated by the particular kind of humiliation that is most abhorrent to her. She, who had once boasted of her promiscuity, now feels the stigma of such a reputation of a "strumpet" or a "whore." Her final cry signifies her union with Antony; she who had scorned and envied Fulvia as "the married woman" now exults in her own marriage in death:

> Husband, I come.
> Now to that name my courage prove my title !
>
> (V. ii. 285)

Antony had given up the god Hercules for her love; for him, she also changes her divinity: "now the fleeting moon/No planet is of mine." To Antony she offers what is most pure in her:

> I am fire and air; my other elements
> I give to baser life.
>
> (V. ii. 287)

Her vision of paradise is as voluptuous as Antony's had been; there is no aspiration except for an eternity of love together. But from this stems an almost mystical contempt for worldly values; as Antony had considered "the world well lost" for a kiss from her, so does she finally resign this world for a kiss from him. What was false once, is true now; her last thought *is* of Antony; without him, why should she stay--Charmian completes the sentence for her--in this "vile world."

In its passions and its generosity, Antony's was a rare spirit; in her death Cleopatra becomes worthy of the isolation that he had endured for her.

REFERENCES

1. A.C. Bradley, "Shakespeare's *Antony and Cleopatra,*" in *Oxford Lectures on Poetry* (London, 1909), p. 291.

2. L.C. Knights, *Some Shakespearean Themes* (London, 1959), p. 147; the phrase is used about the "self-consuming" passion of Antony and Cleopatra. For similar interpretations, see J.F. Danby, "The Shakespearean Dialectic--An Aspect of *Antony and Cleopatra,*" *Scrutiny,* 16 (1949), esp. p. 212, and Derek Traversi, *Shakespeare: The Roman Plays* (London, 1963), esp. pp. 142, 153.

3. Michael Lloyd, "The Roman Tongue." *Shakespeare Quarterly, X* (1959), Maurice Charney, *Shakespeare's Roman Plays* (Harvard, 1961), esp. p. 95, and Ernest Schanzer, *The Problem Plays of Shakespeare* (London, 1963), pp. 138-139.

4. "The Life of Marcus Antonius," quoted from *Shakespeare's Plutarch, ed.* T.J.B. Spencer (Penguin Book, 1964), p. 178; throughout, by "Plutarch".

5. *Ibid.*, pp. 274-275.

6. *Ibid.*, p. 177.

7. For comment on this, see Robert Ornstein, "The Ethic of the Imagination: Love and Art in *Antony and Cleopatra,*" *Stratford-upon-Avon Studies* 8: *Later Shakespeare* (1966), pp. 36-37.

8. Michael Lloyd, *op. cit.*

9. *Op. cit.*, pp. 273-274.

10. Plutarch's Domitius (*ibid,* p. 253) Though it has generally been assumed that this Domitius is identical with the Domitlus Aenobarbus mentioned as Antony's spokesman during the Parthian campaign (ibid., p. 228), this is not absolutely clear from the text, especially in view of the fact that Domitius Aenobarbus is said to have married one of the daughters of Octavia and Antonius (*ibid,* p. 294).

11. *Op. cit.*, p. 199.

12. See Michael Lloyd, "Cleopatra as Isis," *Shakespeare Survey*, 12 (1959), p. 91, and Harold Fisch, "*Antony and Cleopatra*: the Limits of Mythology," *Shakespeare Survey*, 23 (1970).

6

Coriolanus

Coriolanus is somewhat different from the other main tragedies of Shakespeare in many important respects. It is the least metaphysical; the tragic situation is not precipitated by the hero's communion with supernatural forces, nor does he turn in his despair to the heavens for sympathy; he does not even have the protective love of a god, as Antony has of Hercules. Except for the "unnatural scene" with Volumnia and Virgilia, at which "the gods look down," Coriolanus is shown to us in an almost completely political context, and his world is therefore a limited one. However, it would be a mistake to conclude from this that *Coriolanus* is a play in which the chief motive is a clash of interest between the rich and the poor, or between an overbearing Roman aristocrat and reasonable plebeiansh. When Shakespeare choose this little-known story from North's Plutarc, it was not to write a political tract, even though the tragic moment of crisis does turn upon a political situation. Coriolanus takes the political state of Rome seriously, and what he sees around him disturbs him deeply. But even his political views are a facet of a highly personal ethic, the validity and value of which constitute the chief interest of the play. This leads us to the unusual character of the hero. He is not presented as one who is, or has been in the past, loved by the multitude; he has bought no golden opinions from all sorts of people. The first opinions we hear about him are that he is "chief enemy to the people," "a very dog to the commonalty," and that he is proud "even to the altitude of his virtue." To this last charge from the First Citizen, the Second Citizen can only reply: "What he cannot help in his nature you account a vice in him." The first appearance of Caius Marcius tends to confirm the views expressed by the citizens; he is not given any hyperbolical poetry to utter, as Antony is, but only the harsh sounds of:

> What's the matter, you dissentious rogues
> That, rubbing the poor itch of your opinion,
> Make yourselves scabs?
>
> (I. i. 162)

In one long speech, his character is further sketched for us; he will not flatter the citizens whose greatest fault, to him, is their inconstancy:

> Trust ye?
> With every minute you do change a mind
> And call him noble that was now your hate,
> Him vile that was your garland.
>
> (I. i. 179)

This is not mere exposition, but dramatic irony that anticipates the fate of Coriolanus in this tragedy of quickly shifting loyalties. When the Roman citizens call him noble they have first expressed their hate towards him, and when they give him the garland of consulship, it is only to revile him as a traitor a little later.

Plutarch's Coriolanus is, for lack of education, a man "so choleric and impatient that he would yield to no living creature; which made him churlish, uncivil, and altogether unfit for any man's conversation." Further, being too self-willed, he

> remembered not how wilfulness is the thing of the world which a governor of a commonwealth for pleasing should shun, being that which Plato called 'solitari-

> ness'; as, in the end, all men that are wilfully given to a self-opinion and obstinate mind and who will never yield to others' reason but to their own, remain without company and forsaken of all men.

Shakespeare's hero, however, is very differently sketched from Plutarch's boorish orphan deprived of opportunities for a well-balanced education. Though he ultimately suffers the fate of "solitariness" he is not congenitally "unfit for any man's conversation." He has friends among those who, believes, share his noble values; Shakespeare emphasizes the deep regard that Coriolanus has for his friend among the patricians because they are "his fellows in a community of virtue--of a courage, fidelity, and honour, which cannot fail them because they are 'true-bred'.[2] These are the 'heroic' virtues which Coriolanus expects to find in true Romans and, since he finds the citizens destitute of these on every occasion that they are tried, he cannot see how this Hydra deserves a real share in the governance of Rome.

Therefore, there appears an irremediable antagonism between the populace of Rome and Caius Marcius; they resent his pride as much as he scorns their unprincipled conduct. The only quality for which the citizens this hero is his martial valour, though they astutely realize that his triumphs on the battlefield have not been inspired by devotion to his country, but by his desire "to please his mother and to be partly proud." It is significant that in the battle for Corioli, the only battle which is actually staged in the course of the play, he wins his victory *alone;* his title 'Coriolanus' is thus an unpopular one, a humiliating reminder to both Romans and Volsces, though for different reasons. Shakespeare's account of the battle is different from Plutarch's in this detail. The flight of the Roman soldiers is common to both, but in the *Life* Marcus does have a few men to help him.[3] By making his victory a solitary one, Shakespeare heightens the tragedy of this general who leads a nation to battle, but whose honours are not national.

We are never allowed to forget this self-sufficiency of Coriolanus; the word "alone" runs like a refrain through the play.[4] Cominius so completely identifies the triumph of his young friend with his own that there is no trace of envy in his unstinted commendation of Coriolanus for the consulship; he does not realize that his manner of paying tribute may not appeal to the voters:

> Alone he ent'red
> The mortal gate of th' city, which he painted
> With shunless destiny; aidless came off,
> And with a sudden re-enforcement struck
> Corioli like a planet.
>
> (II. ii. 108)

This dazzling splendour of Coriolanus' isolation becomes dulled in the second half of the play, as he comforts his mother when about to leave Rome as an exile:

> --though I go alone,
> Like to a lonely dragon, that his fen
> Makes fear'd and talk'd of more than seen--your son
> Will or exceed the common or be caught
> With cautelous baits and practice.
>
> (IV. i. 29)

Shakespeare deliberately makes these words of Coriolanus ambiguous; the image of the lonely dragon conveys to us simultaneously the banishment as it appears to him, and as it appears to others. Coriolanus has no doubt that even in banishment he will be isolated by the exceptional nature of his deeds, which will, as always, "exceed the common"; the others are filled with a sense of foreboding that Coriolanus in exile will be even more dangerous because removed from the influence of his family and his friends of "noble touch." Further, there is an ironical anticipation of his death at the hands of the treacherous Volsces although Coriolanus here thinks that the only way the *Romans* will ever be able to capture him will be through crafty stratagems. When he leaves Rome next time, he will not leave it alone, but at the head of the Volscian army, with the certainty that he goes to meet his death; in his willingness to pay the price for sparing his native city lies his redemption.

The isolation of this tragic hero results from the complexity of his character; it is the self-consistency of his highly personal values that makes him a Roman hero one day, and a traitorous leader of the Volsces on another. His pride cuts him off from sympathy with his fellow citizens, but at the same time it imposes on him a code of conduct which makes uncompromising demands, and these he does not flinch from meeting. He has no doubt about the rightness of his convictions, and therefore none about the course he pursues to justify them. Unlike Hamlet and Macbeth, Coriolanus--in the first part of the play--faces no tragic dilemma, and that is why he is given no introspective soliloquies. The cardinal values, to him, are constancy and trustworthiness, as we are shown in his first speech to the Roman citizens. His courage in battle is closely associated with this, as also his abhorrence of flattery.

> He can be counted upon in battle to do credit to his noble blood. Since he is not a coward, he does not tell lies, for the liar is a coward afraid to tell the truth; and since he does not tell lies, he flatters no man. Flattery is the weakling's way of gaining favor (sic) and advantage in the world, and the trustworthy man will not stoop to it.[5]

Different facets of this personal ethic of Coriolanus are exhibited in the two parts of this tragedy. In the first part the main interest centres on the relationship between the hero and his social group, finding its climax in the issue of the consulship; the most dramatic moment comes when the election is annulled, and Coriolanus is bamshed from Rome. In the second part, as Bradley points out, the interest of the inward struggle "completely eclipses ... that of the outward conflict."[6] The truly tragic issues arise in this part, with a new battle to be fought, "one of moral forces, culminating in the struggle between Marcius and Volumnia, in which, silently at the last, he accepts defeat."[7]

In no other major tragedy of Shakespeare is there such a rapid and complete reversal in the role of the hero vis-a-vis his social group as in this. With his code of honour based on trustworthiness, it is the slander of being called "traitor" by the contemptible tribunes (III. iii. 65) that makes Coriolanus fall into their trap and provokes him to abuse the plebeians. Yet this proud Roman patrician, in the second part of the play, joins the Volsces against his native country, and becomes a traitor indeed. But if we understand his processes of thought, we must realize that he considers himself an honourable traitor, as Othello regards himself as an "honourable murderer." Granville-Barker is surely right in suggesting that Act IV sc. iii, with its brief vignette of Adrian and Nicanor, two professional traitors, is significantly placed before the appearance of Coriolanus at Antium, so that we may see treason as it is to such soldiers--a matter of mirth and money.[8] What is it that keeps the Roman general from sinking to their level? How is it that he remains capable of the greatest loyalty in spite of the traitorous role that he assumes? The answer lies in his heroic effort to remain true to himself, and the tragedy grows from the clash of loyalties this involves.

In both parts of the play, Shakespeare heightens the tragedy compared with Plutarch's version. In the *Life,* Coriolanus' request to Cominius on behalf of a Volscian prisoner of war is narrated thus:

> 'Among the Volsces there is an old friend and host of mine, an honest wealthy man, and now a prisoner, who, living before in great wealth in his own country, liveth now a poor prisoner in the hands of his enemies; and yet, notwithstanding all this his misery and misfortune, it would do me great pleasure if I could save him from this one danger, to keep him from being sold as a slave.'[9]

In the play the content of the request is significantly different:

I sometime lay here in Corioli
At a poor man's house; he us'd me kindly.
He cried to me; I saw him prisoner;
But then Aufidius was within my view,
And wrath o'erwhelm'd my pity. I request you
To give my poor host freedom.

(I. ix. 82)

Shakespeare makes Coriolanus' sense of obligation much more generous and characteristic by basing it on a brief personal encounter rather than on any friendship of long standing; moreover, his host is a poor man, not a once wealthy citizen. In spite of the fact that this remains only a gesture, because Coriolanus has forgotten his host's name, the wording of the request makes an important dramatic point. We see that, to Coriolanus, the claims of personal loyalty, in this case arising out of kindly hospitality, are more sacred than even the laws of war. And the "pity" felt by him reveals to us, though only for a moment, the "gentler impulses"[10] that lie hidden in the man behind the iron mask. In a minor key, this episode prognosticates his succumbing to his love for his mother, wife and child, the personal emotion overwhelming the soldier's pledge to the Volsces. In the following scene, we see another soldier, Aufidius, and *his* attitude to such values. His hate towards Marcius, he says, will never be softened by any extenuating circumstances:

Where I find him, were it
At home, upon my brother's guard, even there,
Against the hospitable canon, would I
Wash my fierce hand in's heart.

(I. x. 24)

The contrast between the heroic magnanimity of Coriolanus and the petty vengefulness of Aufidius is carefully contrived by Shakespeare at the beginning of the play; the tragedy of Coriolanus at Antium is already implicit here.

Having acquainted us with the highly individual attitudes of Coriolanus, Shakespeare proceeds to the issue of the consulship. This is first hinted at by Volumnia, who seems to have ambitions for her son that we have not seen him share. Her joy in his returning, "the third time with the oaken garland" is heightened by hopes of his elevation in the public world. Shortly before this, we have seen him refuse any reward for his victory at Corioli, and we wonder if the mother understands the son as well as she thinks she does. The difference between Volumnia and Coriolanus is obliquely hinted at as she welcomes him back to Rome, she has lived to see the fulfilment of all her wishes but one, "which I doubt not but/Our Rome will cast upon thee." His reply is terse inits sincerity:

> Know, good mother,
> I had rather be their servant in my way
> Than sway with them in theirs.
>
> (II. i. 192)

Knowing that the price of political office in an elective system is a descent to the values of those who have the votes, he is quite content to gain glory in the martial sphere, where he reigns supreme because of his exceptional valour. He also knows the ritual a candidate for consulship has to go through, and has freely expressed his opinion of it, as Brutus reports:

> I heard him swear,
> Were he to stand for consul, never would he
> Appear i' th' market-place, nor on him put
> The napless vesture of humility;
> Nor, showing, as the manner is, his wounds
> To th' people, beg their stinking breaths.
>
> (II. i. 221)

The "poor gown" of Plutarch has been given a richly symbolic value by Shakespeare the dramatist and actor. The wearning of a gown for a political purpose would easily suggest to him the acting of a part, in a costume donned for the stage, with no relation to, or effect upon, the character of the man wearing it. The irony here lies in the association of the vesture with an abstract quality of character--humility--but nobody suggests to Coriolanus that to become consul he must radically change his character; all that he is asked to do is to act a part. Even Sicinius calls it but a "ceremony," and the 2nd Officer in Act II sc. ii has already pointed out how readily aspirants to political office have pretended to love the common people.

It is exactly this false pretence that is deeply abhorrent to Coriolanus. With his highly individual but deeply sincere code of personal integrity, he finds the ceremony distasteful, and pleads:

> I do beseech you
> Let me o'erleap that custom; for I cannot
> Put on the gown, stand naked, and entreat them
> For my wounds' sake to give their suffrage.
>
> (II. ii. 133)

The image of an actor playing a part, repeated with several variations right up to the end of the play,[11] with the implied dichotomy between thought and action, is meaningfully used by the reluctant candidate: "It is a part/That I shall blush in acting." He, who had never flattered the citizens, to now subject himself to the lie that his wounds were received for the hire of their breath only! He knows, and we know, that it is impossible for him to behave like this; why, then, does he not refuse outright? Once again, he seems to have worked out his own personal solution to the problem; he will behave like an actor who dissociates himself on the stage from the role for which he has been cast. Even so, he feels self-disgust at the sacrifice of his personal integrity involved in the ceremony; the question that he raises is of fundamental importance to the evolution of human society:

> Better it is to die, better to starve,
> Than crave the hire which first we do deserve.
> Why in this wolvish toge[12] should I stand here
> To beg of Hob and Dick that do appear
> Their needless vouches? Custom calls me to't
> What custom wills, in all things should we do't,
> The dust on antique time would like unswept,
> And mountainous error be too highly heap'd
> For truth to o'erpeer.
>
> (II. iii. 110)

During this scene, Coriolanus matures from Volumnia's "boy" to man; though he is no scholar like Hamlet, he has also come to the realization that there is many a custom which is "more honour'd in the breach than the observance." He who knows this, and acts upon this knowledge, must be prepared for isolation from society, since society instinctively clings to the observance of custom for its survival. This is what Coriolanus has to learn now. Resentful of his unflattering way of asking for their votes, the citizens are easily persuaded by the tribunes to annul the election. The family and friends of Coriolanus plead with him to beg the voices of the people once again, this time "mildly"; having listened jto his soliloquy, we know that he will be unable to do so, because the citizens have sunk even lower in his esteem by their latest display of inconstancy. As a political figure, he is at his most eloquent now; however reactionary his creed may seem to us in the abstract, it is entirely vindicated by the events in the context of the play. He sees the ruin of Rome in

> This double worship,
> Where one part does disdain with cause, the other
> Insult without all reason; where gentry, title, wisdom,
> Cannot conclude but by the yea and no
> Of general ignorance--it must omit
> Real necessities, and give way the while
> To unstable slightness.
>
> (III. i. 142)

None attempts to understand the serious implications of what he is saying; the Senators show no grasp of, or interest in, political theory; they are only keen to have 'their' man in power. The tribunes, instead of trying to refute his argument, accuse him of treason; this is ironical because Coriolanus is the only character in this intensely political scene who is willing to put state before self. His furty against the tribunes is only for a moment related to the personal insult; soon, it is directed against them as the destroyers of Roman polity. It should not be too readily assumed that Coriolanus is over-stating his case because of personal pique: it has still to be proved that a healthy society can be collectively constituted of those who are individually unprincipled and corrupt.

In any case, whatever may be the reactions of the modern reader, Shakespeare is carefully trying to place the conduct of his impetuous young hero: this he does through the chorus-like eulogy spoken by Menenius:

> His nature is too noble for the world:
> He would not flatter Neptune for his trident,
> Or Jove for's power to thunder. His heart's his mouth;
> What his breast forges, that his tongue must vent;
> And, being angry, does forget that ever
> He heard the name of death.
>
> (III. i. 255)

Menenius is a shrewd judge of character, whether it be that of his rash protege, or that of the contemptible citizens, or, indeed, his own. He understands the various elements of which the complex nobility of Coriolanus is compounded. This is not indeed the nobility of one who is the "observ'd of all observers"; the qualities of absolute frankness and righteous indignation can easily degenerate into self-willed pride and abuse as they do in the behaviour of Coriolanus. But, in this crisis, where the political and the personal issues are brought to their closest unity, these qualities are noble; his character rises to heroic stature as he tries to define, and live up to, his ideals.

Coriolanus has already offended his partician friends by disregarding their pleas for modernization in his dealings with the citizens; now a deepere tie is threatened by his determination not to be "milder" towards them. He is puzzled and depressed by the differnce on this point between him and Volumnia; as she enters, he asks her what is really the fundamental question:

> Would you have me
> False to my nature? Rather say I play
> The man I am.
>
> (III. ii. 14)

She too seems to want him to assume a role he does not believe in whereas he, like the other major tragic heroes, knows not "seems." When he had tried to assume a false *persona* by donning the gown of humility, his entire being had rebelled against the pretence; ultimately he was unable to be anything but himself. It is this awareness of his self that he wants to be true to, but this mother counsels self-betrayal; you must now speak to the people, she says,

> not by your own instruction,
> Nor by th' matter which your heart prompts you,
> But with such words that are but roted in
> Your tongue, though but bastards and syllables
> Of no allowance to your bosom's truth...
> I would dissemble with my nature where
> My fortunes and my friends at stake requir'd
> I should do so in honour.
>
> (III. ii. 53)

She has apparently brought dissembling and honour into harmony in her system of values, a compromise that is not so easy for her son. Like Gertrude, Volumnia is a platitudinous mother who is not worthy of the son she has borne; the difference is that Hamlet's mother finally realizes her moral inferiority to her son, whereas this forbidding Roman matron never becomes aware of the values her son lives by once he has outgrown her primitive influence. If she had been capable of understanding him, she would have detected, and responded to, the repugnance in her son's words as he yields to her:

> Well, I must do't
> Away, my disposition, and possess me
> Some harlot's spirit!
>
> (III. ii. 110)

Though it is difficult to grant that *Coriolanus* is a satiric play, there is little doubt that Shakespeare is here exposing the double standards of the Roman aristocracy. In terms of social relationships Volumnia would certainly throw up her hands in horror at having to come in contact with bastards and harlots, but at the level of political campaigning she is quite willing to advise her son to father bastard words and to prostitute his honour. Coriolanus' aristocratic code at least has the merit of consistence; the tragedy becomes inevitable when his politic mother succeeds in deflecting him from living by it.

To Coriolanus, his newly discovered identity is very precious, and he is reluctant to violate it. There is yet another moment of recoil, the scene between him and his mother becoming, in some striking ways, parallel to that between Macbeth and his wife before the murder of Duncan. One woman is showing the easy way to consulship, another to a usurped throne. Macbeth's resolve is shaken by Duncan's having honoured him of late, and by his having bought golden opinions from all sorts of people, whereas Coriolanus refuses to buy these opinions at such cost to his own truth. Both men are taunted by the women they love, and yield to emotional appeals from them, without being convinced of the rightness of the actions they advocate. Macbeth knows that he is doomed to wear a false face to hide a false heart, and Coriolanus goes forth in a self-mocking vein, asserting that he will prove a good flatterer indeed!

It is obvious that this resolve of his will be carried out if two factors are constant: his own mood for compromise, and the conciliatory attitude of the tribunes. The first is hardly given a chance; before Coriolanus appears, we listen to the strategy of the tribunes; their plan is to insult and humiliate Coriolanus so that he will forget to be prudent, and give way to his true sentiments. Some critics seem to have ignored this, while blaming Coriolanus for being "an impossible person," or a victim of his own "ungovernable insolence." He makes an uncharacteristic effort to listen to the charges drawn up against him by the tribunes; the only question he asks, in language which has no trace of offensiveness in it, is, why they have dishonoured him by annulling his election as consul. This is the cue Sicinius has been waiting for; he deliberately provokes him by the accusation that he is a traitor to the people. The irony of the charge infuriates Coriolanus; his mother had persuaded him to turn traitor to himself so that he could win the votes of these people; and now to be accused by these cowards and time-servers of treason! Anything now to be true to himself, at whatever cost; for this hero, as for the others, death and exile hold no terrors. The latter is the climax which Sicinius and Brutus have carefully prepared; for these machiavels the drama is performed exactly as rehearsed. The common people also prove good 'extras'; as the sentence of banishment is pronounced, they chant: "It shall be so, it shall be so." Against such a chorus Coriolanus declares proudly: "I banish you." Heroically defiant in misfortune, he does not realize what leaving Rome will mean; that he will learn only in the bitter loneliness of exile.

From this clamour and antagonism, the scene shifts to the moving leave-taking of Marcius from his family and friends. Here he is all tenderness and dignity, as he is when he returns to Rome from Corioli. The Roman world that Shakespeare represents in *Antony and Cleopatra* and *Coriolanus* is aggressively political and masculine; in the former play, it is softened by Cleopatra, in the latter by Virgilia who has often, quite rightly, been compared with Cordelia. The gracious silences between her and her husband provide a still centre not only for him but also for Rome; while others, including Volumnia and Valeria, express their Romanness in action and words, she seems to treasure within herself all the beauty, dignity and virtue of classical Rome. And it is this that her husband cherishes in her though, in her presence, he is rendered inarticulate by the *excess* of the emotion that she arouses in him. As he leaves her, he does not realize that, as a revenge against the perversion of the Roman ideal by the plebeians, he has suffered them to part him from the woman who embodies this ideal in herself. Parted from her, and from the city which has given both of them their ideals, he inevitably becomes "a kind of nothing."

His next appearance, obviously after a considerable time, is dramatic: "Enter Coriolanus, in mean apparel, disguis'd and muffled." There is no doubt that his "mean apparel" is a "grimmer variation" of the gown of humility, as pointed out by Granville Barket; however, there *is* a difference: the present costume of Coriolanus is perfectly consistent with his new state; it is not donned like an actor's costume, as the gown of humility is. It is a literally demeaned Coriolanus that we see, since the noble Coriolanus was destroyed when he was pesuaded to be false to his own nature; he is now a man "who has lost at once his world and his integrity." And since Rome—the Rome of his mother, the patricians and the plebeians—is responsible for the loss of his true identity, he will take his revenge against it by assuming the most un-Roman role possible: "My birthplace hate I, and my love's upon/This enemy town." His speech to Aufidius gives some indication of the way his mind has been working; in sorrow he tells him of his "thankless country," which has left him only the title "Coriolanus":

> The cruelty and envy of the people,
> Permitted by our dastard nobles, who
> Have all forsook me, hath devour'd the rest,
> And suffer'd me by th' voice of slaves to be
> Whoop'd out of Rome.
>
> (IV. v. 74)

The reference to the "dastard nobles" is very significant; he had expected them to share his values, his sense of loyalty to a certain ideal of Rome, but this has not happened. The tragedy of Coriolanus grows now from his blind belief that his own pride is the only value left for him to cherish, since all others have failed him. The interest inthe tragedy now centres on the development of the hero's character to the point where he rejects this unnaturalself-centred glory, and bows to other ties in which great Nature asserts her power.

At first these claims seem to mean nothing to Coriolanus; he leads the Volscian army against Rome "like a thing/Made by some other deity than Nature." But his reaction to the appeal of his once-loved Cominius indicates what it cost him to cleave to his pride and to the Volsces. Coriolanus can hate Rome when he can reduce it to an abstraction; as soon as it is embodied in those he has loved and honoured, he warms to it in spite of himself. We remember how his great love for Virgilia renders him inarticulate; similarly, to be as "nothing" to Cominius chokes him with emotion: as Cominius reports,

> 'Twas very faintly he said 'Rise'; dismiss'd me
> Thus with his speechless hand.
>
> (V. i. 66)

This "gracious silence" is like Virgilia's; at last we see, and Coriolanus is gradually compelled to see, what has bound this husband and wife together; these are depths within his own personality that Coriolanus has not plumbed before, and he is rendered speechless by them; it is his gestures that speak in this supreme moment.

There is another reason why he is reluctant to recognize and express his emotions; he knows that they will undermine his unnatural constancy to his soldier's pledge to the Volsces. His words to Menenius are also a kind of warning to his deeper self which is threatening to overwhelm him:

> Wife, mother, child, I know not. My affairs
> Are servanted to others.
>
> (V. ii. 78)

The tension rises to breaking point as he sees Volumnia, Virgilia, young Marcius, and Valeria appear; their appearance, as always, touches his innermost self and this funds expression in powerful poetry:

> But out, affection !
> All bond and privilege of nature, break !

> Let it be virtuous to be obstinate.
> What is that curtsy worth? or those doves' eyes,
> Which can make gods forsworn? I melt, and am not
> Of stronger earth than others.
>
> (V. iii. 24)

His "instinct" is towards leve, towards the ending of his unnatural isolation, in which he tries to persist and to stand

> As if a man were author of himself
> And knew no other kin.
>
> (V. iii. 36)

He had once before tried to act a part, in the gown of humility, and had been unable to sustain it. By a tragic twist of events and character, he has imposed a much more false role upon himself now, and his true nature breaks through it:

> Like a dull actor now
> I have forgot my part and I am out,
> Even to a full disgrace.
>
> (V. iii. 40)

In his new-found maturity, his mind tries to grapple with more fundamental questions than those of war or politics; as his mother says, he struggles to retain the supremacy of his pride over the pity that draws him towards those he loves. The play had opened with the same charge of pride from a Citizen who had said that all of Caius Marcius' martial exploits were undertaken to please his mother, mother and son seem to have moved away immeasurably from each other since then. He seems impervious to the appeals of this once-proud Roman matron, now broken by her grief on which she has supped alone. In despair, she kneels to him for the second time; the visual parallel to the hierarchical inversion which dramatically expresses the triumph of love over pride in *King Lear* is very striking. At last his pride melts, and he "holds her by the hand, silent."

When he speaks, he has fully grasped the implications of his surrender to "affection"; what exalts him to tragic stature is the heroic defiance with which he reacts to them:

> O mother, mother !
> What have you done? Behold, the heavens do ope,
> The gods look down, and this unnatural scene
> They laugh at. O my mother mother! O!
> You have won a happy victory to Rome;
> But for your son--believe it, O, believe it!--
> Most dangerously you have with him prevail'd,
> If not most mortal to him. But let it come.
>
> (V. iii. 182)

It is doubtful if Volumnia realizes that she is saving Rome at the cost of her son's life; if Coriolanus realizes the imminence of his death, he does not care. His own fate is of no moment now that he has hearkened to the "gods," and has acknowledged the claims of the fundamental relationships of life as part of a divine hierarchy of values.

Simultaneously, Coriolanus tries to be true to his pledge as a soldier, by returning with the Volsces, instead of with the Romans; he has spared his native city, not because he has forgiven in its corruption, but because its true values happen to be enshrined in the Roman women he loves. This subtle distinction is naturally not understood by Aufidius; his treachery provides the epilogue to the great scene between Volumnia and Coriolanus. He knows no honourable code, and easily makes a false charge against Coriolanus: "He watered his new plants with dews of flattery,/Seducing so my friends." The irony here runs deep; Coriolanus was exiled from his nataive country because he could not learn to flatter, and here is Aufidius accusing him of flattering Volscians! We await the inevitable destruction of the self-consistent nobility of Coriolanus when it is at the mercy of the ignoble scheming of his conspiratorial rival.

The scene with the tribunes before the banishment of Coriolanus is repeated when the two generals meet, one affirming his loyalty, the other with assassins ready to stab. The villains in this play leave nothing to chance; their 'traps' for the hero are carefully rehearsed, and they are supremely successful. Coriolanus, like Hamlet, is "most generous, and free from all contriving," and therefore vulnerable to the plotting of machiavels; however, unlike Hamlet, he does not have the consolation of seeing the cunning designs of the machiavels "fall'n on th' inventors' heads." Whereas in the other tragedies exceptional good and exceptional evil are both destroyed and the unspectacular good inherits the earth, in this play *only* the exceptional good is destroyed; the tribunes and Aufidius lose nothing and they learn nothing. With their petty minds, "traitor" to them means a person who does not serve their own selfish interests; they have no idea what such an accusation can mean to one who lives by the ideals of constancy and trustworthiness. When Aufidius makes the charge, and follows it up with the threat to deprive him of his title, "Coriolanus," Caius Marcuius suddenly sees him for the "cur" and "hound" he is--quite appropriately, the kind of abuse he had hurled at the tribunes is revived when there is an equally contemptible object to deserve it. Simultaneous, he has an exhilarating sense of his own personal worth and he makes a defiant assertion of it before the assassins tear him to pieces.

> If you have writ your annals true, 'tis there
> That, like an eagle in a dove-cote, I
> Flutter'd your Volscians in Corioli.
> Alone I did it.
>
> (V. vi. 114)

At the end he glories in the splendour of his isolation, recognizing that, like Julius Caesar in Shakespeare's earliest Roman play, he had bestrid the narrow world like a Colossus, while petty men peeped about to find themselves dishonourable graves. Having redeemed himself by recognizing the bond of nature and by attempting to fulfil his pledge to the Volsces, he is ready to meet death with a constant temper. Unlike Antony, this Roman is denied a death in "the high Roman fashion"; he is alone, on foreign soil, and is butchered by hired assassins.

In spite of his gruesome death, there is no doubt about this hero's nobility. The eulogy at the end, with "noble" as the key word, should be understood with an awareness of its complexity as applied to Coriolanus. The nobility of this proud Roman is not worthy of unqualified admiration, because it is inextricably entwined with limitations of insight, particularly into the value of individual pride.

REFERENCES

1. "The Life of Martius Coriolanus," *Shakespeare's Plutarch,* p. 320-321.
2. A.C. Bradley, *Coriolanus,* British Academy Shakespeare Lecture (1912), quoted from reprint in *Studies in Shakespeare,* British Academy Lectures Selected by Peter Alexander (London, 1964), p. 227.
3. *Op. cit.,* p. 308.
4. For a fuller discussion, see M. Charney, *Shakespeare's Roman Plays,* pp. 176 ff.
5. *Willard Farnham, Shakespeare's Tragic Frontier* (California, 1950), p. 220.
6. *Shakespearean Tragedy,* p. 18.
7. H. Granville-Barker, *Prefaces to Shakespeare* (London, 1963), Vol. III, p. 230.
8. *Ibid.,* pp. 219-220.
9. *Op. cit.,* p. 312.
10. MacCallum, op. cit., p. 581; this remains the most perceptive discussion of the incident.
11. For fuller comment, see Charney, op. cit., pp. 169 ff. See also Una Ellis-Fermor, *Shakespeare the Dramataist* (Loondon, 1961), pp. 69 ff.
12. This emendation of the Folio reading, "Wooluish tongue," does not seem entirely adequate; "wooluish" could easily be a misreading of "wool' nish," as suggested by C. & M. Cowden Clarke, quoted in Furness' New Variorum edition (Philadelphia, 1928), or for "wooliish," as suggested by J. Dover Wilson in

his note in the New Cambridge edition (1960), either of these readings would lend greater point to Coriolanus' contemptuous reference to the citizens as "woollen vassals" (III. ii. 9) with whom he had been forced to identify himself in the gown of humility.

7

Conclusion

The concept of hero in Shakespearean tragedies cannot be fruitfully related to the Aristotelian definition of the ideal tragic hero because the criterion of a "flaw" or "error" which precipitates the tragic situaticn is not central to it. It would seem to be more profitable to trace the origins of the concept back to the world of mythology, in which the hero is "the champion of creative life" and the dragon to be slain by him is "the monster of the status quo." In these tragedies of Shakespeare, the heroic attitude manifests itself in a critical appraisal of the world of custom whereas the non-heroic is identified with an uncritical subservience to this world. The role of the hero is *to ask fundamental questions about the nature of human relationships*; he discovers that he must find the answers for himself, because the other characters are quite content to live by the cliche. In his determination to persist in this search, undeterred by suffering and social ostracism, lies his claim to heroic stature.

Every protagonist (hero) in Shakespeare is of noble rank in his society; as the actioon moves forward, he is denied the privileges which are the concomitants of such a rank. Paradoxically, his inner nobility, which inheres in his integrity, finds expression when all exernal supports are withdrawn; ultimately what unites these heroes is an aristocracy of the spirit. They reject any compromise that involves a sacrifice of their essential principles, and prefer the dignity of isolation to the shoddiness of surrender to a corrupt society. They stand aloof and assess the world that surrounds them; unlike the characters in the Histories and the Comedies, they judge the social judgement which tries to judge them. In creating such characters, Shakespeare transcends the Elizabethan context; as W.G. McCollom has aptly remarked:

> Shakespeare's great tragedies indicate a social attitude far more complex than that which can be derived from oorthodox statements of the Tudor world picture. The work of his tragic period is modern in the sense that it presents man's effort to construct his own values, not in complete independence of traditional concepts of society but with an increasing reliance upon his own awareness, his own experience, and his own ability to interpret human responsibility.[1]

In this effort, the hero receives no encouragement or sympathy; even those closest to him fail to understand why he refuses to follow the conventional codes of conduct. And it is this which causes the greatest anguish to the hero; rejection by society he can face with a certain degree of equanimity, but incomprehension of his attitudes on the part of those whom he loves drives him to the verge of breakdown. The memorable moments in these tragedies are those when failure of rapport first manifests itself. We remember Hamlet bitterly rejecting his mother's pious commonplaces on the deaths of fathers, Macbeth realizing that his wife can retain the natural ruby of her cheeks when his own is blanced with fear, Lear refusing to accept Cordelia's "nothing" and asking her to speak again. In the Roman plays there is the disintegration of Antony when Cleopatra threatens to be unfaithful, and Coriolanus' inability to understand how his mother could want him to be false to his own nature.

Such moments set the tragic process in motion. After these, the hero knows that he is doomed to isolation but, being deeply committed to human relationships, he makes attempts to avoid a complete break. Hamlet, disappointed in his mother, turns to Ophelia for some comfort in the crisis precipitated by the command of his father's ghost; when she too becomes the tool of Polonius and Claudius, he has only Horatio to turn to Macbeth, once he starts committing crimes which are kept secret even from his wife, moves away from the world of the natural into the phantasmagoric world of ghosts and witches; his claim to tragic stature lies in the intensity with which he longs for the restoration of his severed link with humanity. Lear, denied what he regards as his rightful privileges by his daughters, alternately demands and begs what is due to him; only when he is shut out in the storm does he come to an awareness of other bonds with mankind that are possible. In a certain sense Antony is the greediest of all these heroes: he wants Cleopatra as mistress, Fulvia and then Octavia for wife, and he wants to cling to his political alliance with Caesar. One might almost call him a hero in spite of himself; it is not with any elation that he accepts the supremacy of his love for Cleopatra over all his Roman values. But once he has accepted it, he acts with dignity and generosity, he holds no grudge against her for the sacrifices that she has imposed upon him. Coriolanus, totally contrary to his own inclination, tries to please his mother by adopting a conciliatory attitude towards the tribunes whom he holds in contempt. He fails to enact the part that she imposes upon him, and becomes an exile. But when she and his wife come and plead with him to spare Rome, he surrenders to his love for them with the clear knowledge that his life will be the forfeit for the violation of his pledge to the Volsces.

The moment of isolation and seperation is, therefore, also the moment of illumination; the issues at stake are clarified, and decisive choices are made. In making the choice that inevitably means isolation, the hero places primary value upon his own identity and his integrity; this is his heroic quality. Society rejects him for his intransigence, or tries to cajole him to surrender his essential self; he abides by his choice regardless of the consequences. The cost in terms of self-accusation and self-torture is tremendoous, but the hero pays it with dignity; he expresses his anguish only in soliloquy. In their soliloques the heroes analyse themselves and the choices they have made and try to struggle towards self-awareness. In doing this they bring this somewhat clumsy stage convention to its artistic perfection: their intense self-consciousness finds expression in a style which is the high-water mark of Shakespeare's achievement as a writer of poetic drama.

Does the intense individualism of the hero represent a kind of fusion of "the Senecan attitude of Pride, the Montaigne attitude of Scepticism, and the Machiavelli attitude of Cynicism"?[2] The first thing to be noticed in his famous indictment of Eliot's is his loaded use of words--the cavalcade of Pride, Scepticism and Cynicism appears as in a morality play, charged with anti-Christian connotations. And indeed what Elio holds against the Elizabethan hero in general, and the Shakespearean hero in particular, is a lack of Christian humility, the emphasis being placed upon the adjective rather than the noun. Certainly, self-abasement is not a quality of the hero; on the contrary, at some stage of the tragic process, he proudly assets his sense of his own worth. However, even though these heroes do not humble themselves before God or gods, they do bow to those whom they love, and confess their sins before those whom they may have wronged. We remember Lear kneeling to Cordelia, and Coriolanus breaking down before his kneeling mother; we remember also the apology of Hamlet to Laertes, of Macbeth to Macduff, of Antony to the soldiers he has dishonoured. Eliot's cavalcade of Vices follows the wrong characters; Pride, Scepticism and Cynicism characterize the villains and their underlings in these plays. Claudius is unable to pray, Goneril and Regan deny the privileges of fatherhood, Octavius regards a sister as an asset expendable in the interest of politics, and Aufidius is guilty of brutal treachery against an honourable enemy. In the human world these heroes atone for their sins: the rest is silence.

Intense self-awareness as a tragic quality emerges slowly in the plays of Shakespeare.[3] In the independence of Romeo's attitude to the family feud between the Montagues and the Capulers, Shakespeare attempts to give him something of the individuality of the latter tragic heroes. Romeo is the only character in the play who admits his indifference to the feud in public, and to a member of the other family, Tybalt. Romeo and Juliet do not ask fundamental questions about the nature of human relationships, but their love does make them rise above the conventions of the Verona in which they live, to wonder: "What's in a name?" But their characterization is not mature enough to carry such exploration very far. Their death heals a social breach, but we do notfeel that their personalities have made a powerful impact on their social *milieu.* Their love, like Juliet's beauty, is "too rich for use, for earth too dear!" It is expressed in exquisite poetry which creates a world of its own and has no point of contact with the idiom of Verona. The social and the personal emotions touch tangentially, and are not inextricably entwined as they are in the later love tragedy, *Antony and Cleopatra.* Like the later tragic heroes, Romeo is banished, but his banishment is not directly related to his repudiation of the taboos of Verona. Moreover, his exile is seen in entirely external terms, dictated by the exigencies of the plot, and not as the starting point of a process of self-discovery.

In *Julius Caesar,* Brutus has some of the qualities of the tragic hero, and is set apart from the other conspirators against Caesar by the idealism of his motivation. However, Brutus falls short of the stature of a tragic hero because of his failure, (or that of his creator), to fully explore the consequence of his involvement in the murder of Caesar. We can believe that he could contemplate the deed without realizing its implications in personal terms, but the commission of it should have transformed him, as it transforms Macbeth. Brutus, in the second half of the play, is too externally conceived to be regarded as a tragic hero. His stoicism is, in fact, a barrier against his feeling things as a man: the murder of Caesar and the suicide of Portia reveal no hidden depths of his personality to us. Brutus, thoough undoubtedly noble, is not tragic because he does not suffer enough.

It is in *Hamlet* that Shakespeare achieves a striking success in portraying the tragic potentialities of a cleavage between a society and its most noble individual. If we want to see how far removed is Shakespeare's concept of the hero from that of his contemporaries, we have only to look at the Laertes-like heroes of other revenge plays, who go about like raving maniacs crying "Vindicta mihi!" in the true Senecan manner. The distinctively Shakespearean tragic note is sounded in the soliloquies of Hamlet: the focus shifts from the nature of action to the nature of the agent of action. There are no neat formulae here; we are shown a man alone, trying to work out his own solution to the problem of relating his aspirations and ideals to those that society tries to impose upon him.

For almost a decade, Shakespeare seems fascinated by the kind of tragedy that is born of the clash between an exceptional, unbending hero, and a society that wants to reduce him to its own shabby standards. He depicts situations of varying complexity--Hamlet resisting not only Claudius but also the spirit of his dead father, Lear losing the world of Goneril and Regan only to find the world of Cordelia, Antony breaking with Caesar and winning an enternity of love with Cleopatra, Coriolanus rejecting Rome and then saving it at the cost of his life. The hero is pitted against overwhelming odds and, at the physical level, he is broken and destroyed. But, at the spiritual level, he triumphs through the dignity with which he endures the consequences of his choice. However, secular Shakespeare's tragedies may be, one cannot avoid describing the hero in paradoxes of almost Pauline significance.

The heroes of Shakespeare are the real heroes of society. The hero of Shakespeare is always facing ideological clashes. They are the incarnation of justice. Where justice is denied the heroes of Shakespeare indulge in actors and waging ferocious battle for the noble cause of justice. The heroes of Shakespeare are symbolic in character. Hence we can conclude that the heroes of Shakespeare is living in their style and imaginations which always bring a moral lesson and value to the society as a whole.

REFERENCES

1. *Tragedy* (New York, 1957), p. 199.
2. T.S. Eliot, "Shakespeare and the Stoicism of Seneca," Shakespeare Association Lecture (1927); cited from reprint in *Shakespeare Criticism* 1919-35 (World's Classics, 1936), Selected by Anne Bradley (later Mrs. Ridler), p. 216.
3. See H.V.D. Dyson, *The Emergence of Shakespeare's Tragedy*, British Academy Shakespeare Lecture (1950).

Index

❑❑❑